LIVE LIFE

BUT LEARN TO LIVE YOUR LIFE

by

Larry D Snell

larrydsnellbooks@gmail.com **larrydsnellbooks.com**

LCCN: 2025902876

Hardback ISBN: 978-1-967178-01-8

Table of Contents

ABOUT AUTHOR

Larry Dwayne Snell (Born July 22, 1965)

I was born in San Bernardino, California, then moved to Detroit in 1973. I attended Mackenzie High School in the 1980s before transferring to Cody High School. Due to unforeseen circumstances, I left school to become very familiar with the city of Detroit and started living my life.

Eventually, I went back to school and graduated from Wayne County Community College with a liberal arts degree in humanities, then received a bachelor's degree in journalism from Wayne State University on a scholarship.

I worked as an Assignment Desk Editor and writer for WXYZ-TV 7 News Detroit for seven years, then accepted the Assignment Desk Editor/Writer position at WJRT-TV 12 News in Flint, Michigan. Three years later, I moved back to Detroit as an Assignment Desk Editor/Writer with WDIV-TV News 4 in Downtown Detroit for three years.

I then pursued an education degree and taught grades 4 through 6 at George Washington Carver Academy for four years. I also served as the MEAP Assistant Coordinator there.

I took some master's courses while being accepted into the Griots program at Marygrove College to pursue a master's degree with a combined Early Childhood Education focus, but I became overwhelmed with the accelerated courses.

I then served as Project Manager for Detroit Parent Network for two years. Later, I worked for a few automotive suppliers as a purchaser and a Case Processing Manager.

I adore people ... I love animals ... I lust for life ... but I find the ultimate satisfaction in sharing the life that was meant for me.

CHAPTER I –
THE CONFUSION & DYSFUNCTION

My buddies assumed I had the best childhood ever. We did everything, from building go-carts and racing down the block; to making cap guns and slingshots and having shootouts in the neighborhood. We had so much fun.

There were rarely any disagreements or altercations. And when there were, I had five brothers who were extremely overprotective and served as deterrents to any bullying toward me. However, I kept all my disputes from them. I hated trouble and getting them involved in my issues.

I exhibited a lot of genuine love and optimism about life. I assumed everyone embodied that same compassion and commitment toward life. My outward appearance must have given the impression of the happiest kid in the world. However, the outward appearance was misleading. I had internal struggles that consumed a lot of my childhood while growing up in Detroit.

My dad would have arguments with my mother, and my brothers always took her side. He sometimes accused her of cheating with a man who was a member of her Gin Rummy group. The group gambled every Wednesday night at different locations. I would see this man and think, *He's certainly not her type*. But my father thought so. Because of this, he was miserable at times, then got drunk and instigated arguments. This escalated when the games were over.

My father insisted this man never come back to our home again – and he never did. However, he would show up at the other locations where they played. I knew because my little sister and I would sometimes accompany my mother to the other locations. My father urged her to take us along and requested that she leave the parties early. It was his way of keeping an eye on her.

After twenty-five years of marriage and ten kids, if the affair was true, my dad had every right to be a little jealous and overprotective.

My brothers always sided with my mom, and they would sometimes go way beyond the normal boundaries to protect her. These altercations sometimes got physical.

Their actions scarred me for life. I will never forgive, forget, or understand how or why they got into physical altercations with my dad.

I could see the devastation on his face after the fights with my brothers. I guessed this was a pivotal time in his life, and he couldn't fathom why this—*an act of defiance by his own sons*—was happening. His offspring were now seriously challenging his manhood. Even as a nine-year-old, I remember thinking there was no excuse for such behavior from a son directed toward his father. I was a tiny kid and remember crying and begging my mom to make them stop. I harbored a silent hatred within me toward my brothers.

I remember thinking to myself, this man takes us hunting (I hated it), ice fishing (I hated it), and would often sneak around the back of the house, scaring the hell out of us while we played Gin Rummy together some nights. He got a kick out of making us scream in fear. Afterward, he would come into the house and laugh hysterically. We couldn't help but laugh with him. He had a great but twisted sense of humor and lived for his kids … and a bottle of liquor. Other than his accusations against my mom, he was the happiest drunk I had ever seen.

And now this! It was strange to see these altercations between him and my brothers.

I knew he'd do anything for us, and we'd do anything for him. So, the fights were not only devastating to me - they also frightened me. Once, I was home alone with my parents, and they got into a heated argument. I must have been about ten years old at the time. I cried, knowing if they fought, I could do nothing. I was the youngest and the smallest. And like clockwork, it escalated. I cried and watched, then he struck her. I got so emotional that I acted out on impulse.

My instincts took over. I leaped on his back, crying like a newborn. He stopped hitting her and looked at me. The look on his face was pure shock. I could almost read his expression: *Not you too!* He must have thought. That shocked look on his face told me everything—like

my brothers, he assumed that I was there to fight him in defense of my mother as well.

But to his surprise, I hugged his neck as tightly as I could. I kissed his cheek as I continued to cry. His shocked expression turned into a look of puzzlement. He gazed into my eyes with the weirdest look.

Just then, I said, **"Please don't hit my momma like that,"** and I hugged him even tighter. He raised up—his eyes suddenly went watery. He sat me on the couch and went to bed. My love and concern for the two of them had gotten through. He never raised a hand to my mother again.

My household had become normal. My parents began taking us to the Eastern Market with them every weekend. I remember being so happy seeing so much newfound love between the two of them. From that moment on, we began doing everything as a family again.

Seven years later my dad died of cancer just before his 52nd birthday. I was seventeen years old.

CHAPTER II –
FINDING MYSELF

It wasn't until high school that I found some semblance of my comfort zone – I loved playing sports. When I explored different sports, I surprised myself with how athletic I was. I became athletically in tune with myself and played different sports daily. In junior high school, a classmate was the talk of the school when he jogged around the track field so many times (equivalent to 7 miles). His accomplishments were announced over the PA system. He was a future track star. I thought to myself, I could outdo that mark if I wanted.

So, after school, I went back to the school's track field and ran around the track twice as many times as he did. Of course, there was no write-up or principal announcement broadcast over the PA system. But I did it. I only did it to prove my point to myself. Besides, I liked basketball. And in high school, I would eventually get to join the team. When tryouts were held for the varsity and junior varsity basketball teams at Mackenzie High, I was convinced that I'd make the team, so I stayed after school for the tryouts. Despite my short stature, I was quick. Hell, I'd played in the local PAL League and saved our team from the biggest loss of the season with 17 points, 11 rebounds, and 2 assists, and I was only 5'6".

I was sure I would at least make the team—at least junior varsity squad. But my nerves got the best of me before walking into that gymnasium. The school was nearly empty after seventh-hour classes. The only occupants were the students trying out for the teams.

I was nervous and paced back and forth outside in the hallway, trying to work up the courage to go into the gymnasium and give it a shot. I knew I could do it. I tried hard to convince myself not to be discouraged. I finally resolved to go in and *just do it*. But then, at that very moment, when I turned to enter the gymnasium, my brother, *Old Man*, coincidentally turned the corner. He looked me up and down in a condescending kind of way, as if I was out of place, and asked me what I was doing.

I told him I was going to try out for the basketball team. He let out prolonged schmuck laughter, then paused and said, ***"You must be kidding. You won't make the team,"*** he continued. ***"Those giants will make a fool out of you on that court."*** His smug laughter continued as I walked off. I decided not to try out for the team.

I never considered how influential he was over me, but rather how unsure I allowed myself to be regarding my own potential. I let his words discourage me. I left the tryouts that day feeling inadequate. If I could tell my younger self something at that moment in time, I would've told myself: Never allow someone to discourage you from attempting to succeed ... Never allow someone else to stunt your progress ... Never accept failure without trying to succeed. I should have screamed to my inner self, "*Just do it ... Nothing ventured, nothing gained,*" but I didn't.

I was only 5'6" at the time. But I grew five more inches and eventually made the team two years later. But I wasn't as confident or as eager as I had been years earlier. Had I not been dissuaded earlier in my freshman year, maybe my confidence would have soared through the roof. Maybe I could have ridden that momentum to success - maybe even graduated and gotten a scholarship or soared to even greater achievements. Just maybe, I could have even competed against or with Michael Jordan for championships. Sure, it's far-fetched - But you never know.

CHAPTER III –
MY FIRST REAL ENCOUNTER

For years, I found comfort playing basketball on Cody High's outdoor courts during my homeroom class. The real athletes and academic maniacs were slaving away in the classrooms while I wasted away having fun. Unfortunately, it would be another two years before truant officers enforced class participation. I spent most of my high school days skipping school, honing my basketball skills outside the classroom on school property. There were no fans to criticize me when I double-dribbled or missed a shot terribly. I was comfortable without the criticism that came with not being the best.

We played ball and hung around Cody High School until 3:15 p.m.— after the last hour dismissed. Years of the most vital times in my life were being wasted. I was clueless about how this decision would affect my life.

I had fallen a grade behind and was shocked. I didn't know why I was so surprised. I missed fifty school days in a two year period. However, I was willing to play catch-up despite the embarrassment. I was willing to show my face in a sophomore classroom while my junior peers passed me in the hallways in disbelief. I knew for a fact that I was smart enough to catch up and keep up. I just never had the motivation to apply my knowledge.

This setback was self-inflicted. I shamed and humiliated myself all on my own. And now, here I was - I finally made the junior varsity basketball team while playing catch-up and was trying to put my life back together. But then, one very eventful day changed the trajectory of my life. It changed more drastically than I could have ever imagined.

As our seventh hour class dismissed, my friend Kendall and I took our usual route home. We noticed we were being trailed by a group of guys. Mostly all the students took this route home, so I wasn't really concerned about these guys. There were so many of them that I assumed they were students.

Besides, nearly all my older brothers were already done with school and were hustling and dealing in that general vicinity except

Hickey. He was the only one of us boys who graduated from high school and went straight to the military. *Old Man* hadn't become the neighborhood kingpin just yet, but he knew a lot of guys. So, there was no need to be concerned about this group who were following us.

Just as I had eased my concerns, three of the boys from the group pounced on my back while my buddy watched in undeniable fear. Although I had been tackled and my coat ripped off me, I'll never forget the look on Kendall's face while I looked up from the snowy lawn. He was terrified, but we were still intact. They simply wanted my coat - a Max Julian that my sister had given me for Christmas or something. I was never into that flashy stuff. However, I didn't think the coat was too ostentatious to warrant that kind of violent attraction. But it was expensive and had fur around the collar, so a lot of people in fashion knew what kind of coat it was.

I think the fur drew the attention of the criminals. I guess I was **flexing** because it certainly made me look more materialistic than I was. Thinking back, it reminds me of Denzel Washington in the movie **American Gangster.** His Puerto Rican wife (not truly knowing his character) gifted him the chinchilla coat and hat that he wore it to the fight. It drew the unwanted attention that began the start of his dissension. Maybe I should have burned the Max Julian or simply turned it down.

When the group got what they wanted, they left. One of the girls from school, who witnessed the whole incident, caught up with us. The girl informed us that she knew who the boys were and provided

9

the leader's government name as well as his alias. She even said he lived on her block.

As she provided this information, my heart pounded with true fear. The fear wasn't from having to see the boys again. I was more fearful about my brothers finding out that I got robbed. This was serious and could get very ugly, really fast. I contemplated not telling them at all. I just wanted to figure out a way to get the coat back.

I swore Kendall to secrecy before we got on our block. I had five brothers, and I knew what getting them involved could mean. The brother that I really didn't want to get involved in this mess was Steve. He had no patience, expressed very little reasoning, and had absolutely no fear whatsoever of confronting anyone.

We turned on our block and walked toward my house. Kendall lived across the street. Coincidentally, when we got to the area of the block where Kendall crossed, we saw *Steve*. It was as if my heart dropped to my stomach.

Kendall exclaimed, in excitement, *"Your brother just got robbed!"* I looked at Kendall and said, *"What the* fuck *did you do that for?"* but he never looked at me as he provided the details to *Steve*. I had a gut feeling that this was going to turn disastrous ... and it did.

I was obligated at this point to provide the address the girl had given me to *Steve*. Kendall asked me if I wanted him to ride. I told him, *"Hell no,"* and sarcastically added, *"You've done enough."*

Steve demanded I take him where the guy lived. He loaded a shotgun and made me ride to the house. As we reached the house, he banged on the door with five rapid knocks. A woman answered through the door without opening it. *Steve* demanded the woman go get *Slick* (as the guy was known) and have him come outside. The woman claimed she was the only one home. He then demanded in an impatient voice, *"I'll be back at 5:30, and Slick better be here, and he better have that coat when I come back."* The woman answered, *"Okay."*

Like clockwork, *Steve* and I returned at 5:30, and the coat hung over the porch banister of the home, but this time no one ever came to the door. I prayed they wouldn't as *Steve* again knocked rapidly on the door.

I thanked *Steve*, hoping this was all over, and reminded him that no one hit me when they robbed me. But he wanted to know who *Slick* was. So, during his own investigation, he found out where *Slick* and his gang hung out, but he didn't know what he looked like.

About three days later, *Steve* asked me to come to the arcade at the corner to identify *Slick*. I warned *Steve* that *Slick* always had a gang with him, and his gang traveled in packs like hyenas. I tried to discourage him. I warned him that they would know I was his brother, and that if he did anything, those guys would find a way to kill me later.

This deterrent strategy didn't work. But *Steve* assured me that he wouldn't do anything in the arcade. He promised to lower his cap over his face so they wouldn't recognize him as my brother. I trusted him

to simply talk to the guy. Five minutes earlier, *Steve* had placed a sawed-off shotgun by the tree adjacent to the arcade. Therefore, I was hopeful that nothing would escalate inside the arcade.

We entered the arcade. I recognized Slick immediately. I thought to myself, *"Don't nod,"* but as I looked at Slick, I turned to see *Steve*, and he was looking right at me, so I did the unthinkable, I nodded and left the arcade. I don't think there was ever a conversation between them in that arcade. I had barely gotten out of the door before I (and twenty of *Slick's* boys), as well as others, witnessed *Steve* running out the door behind *Slick* … they were running in the middle of Plymouth Road during rush-hour traffic. *Steve* was chasing him. They didn't seem to pay much attention to the cars zooming past them on both sides of Plymouth Road. *Slick* ran as fast as he could, but he couldn't outrun *Steve*.

Steve never had to get the shotgun … hell, he never had time. He reached around, and in rapid action, he was slapping *Slick* in the mouth with a policeman's issued Slim Jim as he chased him. Blood was pouring from *Slick's* mouth as he ran. *Steve* had that Slim Jim in his back pocket when he entered the arcade. I never even noticed it.

There were two things I recognized immediately during this incident: First: *Slick* couldn't outrun *Steve*, so this beating took place in the middle of rush-hour traffic for what seemed like forever. It went from the arcade eastbound on Plymouth Avenue at Asbury Park all the way to St. Mary's Street and Plymouth Road. Second: *Slick* had a gang of about twenty-five guys with him in that arcade … and they watched my 5'8" brother humiliate their leader in broad daylight, in front of everyone there, and didn't do anything.

I knew there was going to be retaliation … there had to be after such embarrassment and humiliation! On Monday morning, I got about three phone calls from elderly ladies on my block advising me not to go to school that day. They explained that about thirty boys waiting on the corner of my street saying they were going to kill me.

That incident basically marked the beginning of the end of my high school experience. I transferred schools, but nothing was ever the same again. I moved from the neighborhood and started the second chapter of my life.

CHAPTER IV –
NOT SLICK AGAIN!

I avoided *Slick* at all costs. I left the neighborhood to live with my sister. After a while, I had established some street credibility myself. I had friends who were willing to protect me at all costs. They were dropouts too and always assured me that they would do anything for me. I was no longer that frightened little schoolboy. I skyrocketed to 6'2" to go with my street reputation. Although I had a gang after me, I was now a force to be reckoned with. However, I was still hoping I didn't run into *Slick*. I didn't hang out with as many guys as he did, but we had enough people and guns to defend ourselves if he ever tried anything. Although I no longer lived in that neighborhood, I frequently returned there to establish part of my hustle. Therefore, I was in and out of that neighborhood many times.

About two years later, I visited the neighborhood to collect some money and stopped at the supermarket for a soda or something. As I stood in line to pay, I noticed two guys in line behind me. One of them said, **"Hey, what's up?"** I looked and noticed it was *Slick*. I nodded and responded in a low tone, **"Sup?"** I always carried a gun but didn't on this day. I couldn't run. I thought it would show fear and trigger a reaction from them.

I noticed none of his boys were standing outside the store, so I knew I had a 50-50 chance of getting away had I chosen to run. Surprisingly, he didn't seem as threatening to me anymore, so I paid for my items and walked toward the exit. I checked my peripheral while plotting a run-route for when I got out of the store - just in case. Just then, the most amazing thing happened.

As I reached for the car door, he was coming out of the store with his buddy and said, **"Take it easy, man."** I replied, **"You too, Slick!"**

That was the last time I ever saw *Slick*. I thought to myself, I'd moved schools and later dropped out because of this guy. And after finally seeing one another following all that drama, we greeted each other as old friends. It was like tossing a grenade that turned out to be a dud.

A couple of years after that incident, *Slick* got into an altercation with one of the neighborhood mechanics. The mechanic, *Coffee*, rebuilt

and rented out old classic cars for money to the neighborhood drug dealers. *Slick* accused *Coffee* of making shoddy repairs on his car and wanted a refund. *Coffee* told him to bring the car back so that he could repair it correctly, but *Slick* wanted a refund and warned him that if he didn't get it, he'd come back and *handle that shit*.

Well, he did come back and shot and killed everyone who was there. In all, about four people were killed at *Coffee's* house on Mansfield Street that day. The local news covered the story. I knew *Coffee*, so I'd heard about the story on the local news, but I never knew who pulled the trigger. Years later, *Old Man* confirmed to me that *Slick* was the trigger man and was later arrested on multiple counts of murder.

I had often rented cars from *Coffee* when I traveled to Florida. I thought how ironic it was that *Slick* had killed him and his friends that day. He was a madman. I counted my blessings.

CHAPTER V –
MY EXPLORATION BEGINS

I later moved to Highland Park with my older sister. This was a fresh start. She and her husband had a nice house on Monterey Street. I remember all the things that took place at the Howard Johnson's on the corner at Woodward Avenue and Monterey Street. It was like a scene from *American Gangster* every day. There were pimps, whores, drug dealers, and all types of hustlers at that corner.

I often walked to the store and saw some of the most beautiful women I'd ever seen working the streets. Woodward Al, as he was known, used to pay me ten dollars to keep an eye on his women while he left for about twenty minutes. I was young. I think he took a liking to me because he knew my brother-in-law, who dealt heroin.

My sister's husband, *Chucky,* was the heroin king. He moved mounds of it. *Old Man* got involved first, and it didn't take long before I started dealing as well. I had only heard about the heroin game and never knew where it existed. Up until then, I only ever moved a little weed every now and then, but now I was moving heroin. And heroin was a different beast—I had never dealt or seen heroin before. This was an extreme and more dangerous kind of hustle—a game synonymous with murder, overdose, and corruption. But ironically, it was very lucrative. My brother-in-law, who was once a star college football running back, before blowing out a knee, was a master at this game and made a small fortune.

I watched him crush quinine and dorm pills into a bowl, then sieve uncut heroin into the mixture. He then packaged it in tiny envelopes stamped: ***Blue Magic***. I never knew the significance of that name for that product until I saw *American Gangster* decades later. Apparently, the addicts did because Chucky got rich quick with his trademark brand.

There were **_three_** incidents in the heroin game that changed the trajectory of my hustle in this street game. We'll get to them shortly, but first, let's focus on my entrance.

My brother-in-law was a true hustler. On occasion, he promoted concerts at local venues with some big-name entertainers. Some of the

Motown legends would be at our house. I would often see a Checkered Cab parked outside our house for hours. When I went downstairs, I'd catch glimpses of these singing legends getting high as a kite. They would sniff heroin and relax on the sofa for hours prior to performing at the Centennial Building, Fox Theatre, or the Opera House. The cab obviously had the meter running while they indulged. Upon seeing this, I assumed there were no limits to Chucky's customer base. And just like him, the success and ascension of my rise would depend on my customer base and how much *smack* I could move.

Watching and following *Old Man's* lead, I became truly acclimated to the streets. I was no longer in the minor league but the majors. I still had minor league talent, though. But what mattered was my connection, and I had a personal conduit to as much **Blue Magic** as I could move and a cousin who was willing to be the eyes and ears in my blind spots. He was willing to put anyone down who confronted me. He was awesome … I had someone I could trust, and that meant a lot because I was still learning this game but knew, not everyone could be trusted.

I had five older brothers as well. Besides my oldest and military boy, they were hustlers long before I entered the game. So, the blueprint was there. *Steve* (Mister Fearless) was a pimp (not just figuratively). He moved heroin as well and, to his demise, eventually used it. He had beautiful women working for him just like Woodward Al.

For the longest time, I simply thought he had a lot of girlfriends because it seemed all women thought he was handsome and liked him. I remember seeing these girls and thinking I could marry a girl like one of his girlfriends. I was naïve as hell.

Steve had a different girl every other night. They were gorgeous, but when I learned what his hustle was about, I wasn't interested in following his lead.

He was more of my protector, and I admired that about him. But he hustled these beautiful women, and I hated that about him. I hated the way he treated his women. I remember about four or five of the most gorgeous women I had ever seen bringing him food and money whenever he was around. They always brought him things as some sort of peace offering after he'd reprimanded them for one reason or

another. I remember thinking to myself ... I could never take these women for granted.

But all good things come to an end. His world came crashing down on him when he fell in love with one of his women. At some point, she came to her senses and left him. He was heartbroken. I'd never seen him like that before. He made some very costly decisions afterward. He began using his own product, served more than two decades in prison, and eventually died. I was devastated.

When I think of him, I sometimes picture him spreading pepper in our backyard and down the alleyway behind our house to throw off the scent of the police dogs attempting to track him down. He then jumped into the back seat of my dad's broken Buick parked in the driveway. Police were looking for some guys who'd robbed a jewelry store and Steve was seen in the area and fled the scene.

Five minutes later, police had the neighborhood on lock-down. Turns out, two other guys robbed the jewelry store, and *Steve* robbed them. He truly dodged a bullet that night. My mom, bless her heart, knew he had jumped in that car and was in some sort of trouble. However, she had no idea why they were looking for him. I remember her telling the police, who were questioning residents, that she hadn't seen anyone.

I wonder, had my father been home, if he would have turned my brother in. He didn't play that. And as far as he was concerned, we should have been in the military after high school anyway.

Steve ended up spending most of his adult life in prison. He was released after nearly 30 years of incarceration, but the adjustment proved to be too much. I lost him about five years after his release. And to this day, of the ten of us, he is the only sibling I have ever lost. It's still hard to think about him. Regardless of how he lived his life, I always remember that handsome teenage kid who performed a perfect rendition of James Brown in front of my parents and their friends. I remember him trying to play all these instruments like *Prince*. He even looked a little like *Prince*. In another life, had he been afforded more opportunities, he could have been an entertainer.

Then, there was *Beast Boy*. He wasn't the brightest bulb in the pack as a teenager. He was in and out of jail for petty crimes. But his stints were never more than two to three years at a time. I never aspired to follow his leadership. He hung out with a group of guys who were known for terrorizing other hustlers. His friends were murderers and

had a hell of a reputation in Highland Park. They were like the *Young Boys Incorporated* (YBI) before **they** appeared on the street scene.

The leader of *Beast Boy's* group was a well-known guy named *Skip*. He drove a white Mercedes Benz—I hadn't known many dealers driving a 500 SEC Benz. And he was a force to be reckoned with on the streets. I didn't know much about *Skip*, except that he sold a lot of cocaine. Later, I went on a few double dates with his younger brother, *Sean*. He liked my cousin, and I liked her friend. I barely knew *Sean*, and I was shocked to be hanging out with him so much. Turns out he was a murderer and died by the same sword. Years later, I heard that *Skip* was knocking on drug dealers' doors looking for crack. He later died of an overdose. That irony was almost palpable.

Beast Boy formed a reputation as a stingy guy who had dope fiends knocking at his living room window. He sold crack right out of his living room window. Discretion was not a part of his hustle. There was nothing "low-key" about this guy. It puzzles me how long he lasted in the game. Narcotics officers raided his house on several occasions. I was relieved that they never threw the book at him. I guess he was lucky and a bit more clever than I gave him credit for being. He eventually got out of the game and made the most of it.

What's weird is, he had a child with one of his girlfriends. Turns out, he was a great dad - one of the best. He did anything for his little girl. He started working a real job because he wanted to be there for her. I truly believe that kid changed his world.

He and his baby's mom argued and fought more than any couple I had ever known. They would go as far as busting each other's car windows during their violent brawls. Surprisingly, they were always back together by the end of the day. Their relationship was puzzling and stupid to me. Every time she assumed he had an affair; they were at it.

I got the impression he liked violent women for some reason. Prior to this one, he dated *Sonya*. She was streetwise as hell and had her own hustle. She bought *Beast Boy* everything, and he loved it. I think he really liked her, and I liked *Sonya*. She seemed like a happy-go-lucky woman who calmed him.

When she stopped coming around, I wondered what happened. Then I found out that she had been raped, beaten, and found murdered in an abandoned house on Detroit's west side.

Once *Beast Boy* turned his life around, he surprisingly approached me for advice. He said his in-laws had gotten him an interview with Ford Motor Company working as a Hi-Lo driver, but only part-time. His current job was at a factory where he was provided benefits, but it appeared to be a dead-end job. And he needed those benefits so that his daughter had insurance coverage. He wanted my advise on taking the part-time job.

I was so proud of him. I appreciated his turnaround. He began to exhibit role model qualities - in a sense. Even though it was a labor job, I encouraged him and hoped he would pursue the Ford job. I appreciated how he treated his kid and hoped things would go smoothly for him.

I based my encouragement on the following:

The Frederick Douglass mentality or approach toward the survival of Black people in America never really appealed to me. I always admired the *W. E. B. DuBois'* approach. I felt like we had something to prove. Don't misunderstand me, I'd done a lot of labor and was considered the best at it. And earning a living through defined labor duties is fine. But only if you can approach your daily labor duties in a way that eases your workload without sacrificing production … always approach the job searching for ways to ease your labor output and pursue different skills to make yourself more valuable. Otherwise, you'll be considered a mule.

My reply was biased. Maybe it was because I was a gambler. I advised him to take the part-time job. I told him if Ford decided to bring him in full-time with benefits and eventually hire him, the reward would be an improvement. And judging from his relationship with his daughter and his volatile girlfriend, he was going to need that larger benefit package. I prayed that Ford world bring him in full-time—they did. He has been there ever since.

Then there's *Old Man*. We had grown close because of our age and similarities. He was only a year older than I. And boy, was he lucky. He always won at gambling, hit the lottery occasionally, and women loved him. In fact, he was loved by everyone at our school. If there was a

Homecoming King for elementary school, he would have won, hands down.

People seemed to respect and love him wherever he went. We called him *Old Man* because of the way he walked and also because he always seemed wiser than his years.

Looking back, I think he was unaware or simply ignored the impact he had on my life. His criticisms and actions affected me tremendously. I think back on my high school basketball days when he'd shaken my confidence. At one point, he even caused the breakup of my seventh-grade girlfriend, *Nikki*.

She was my first girlfriend and my first kiss as well. She could have been my wife and the mother of my kids. I was devastated about our breakup, but *Old Man* teased and embarrassed me for dating her because of her imperfections.

I saw *Nikki* years later. She had just been released from prison. She served a ten-year sentence for drug possession charges. I heard the initial sentence was five years, but once there, she beat a girl so badly in prison that they tacked on another five years for assault. I may have dodged a bullet. Maybe it was good that *Old Man* teased me for dating her and caused that breakup.

Now I was following his lead. *Blue Magic* was our product, and it was in demand. I now had relatives on my small payroll. They just wanted to be a part of the movement. I don't know if anyone truly believed we'd be millionaires. We were just beginning our shameful profession of community destruction, self-hatred, and social ostracism. But my gosh, it was fun.

Hustling in Highland Park was tough. There was a lot to learn. Lesson one was to watch out for *Officer Jackson*. He didn't take you to jail, but he would take your dope and beat you so badly that you were hospitalized. At least once a week, you would hear about these incidents happening.

I wondered how he had gotten away with it for so long. But then I realized that he took their money and dope, and dealers would rather **suck up** the losses rather than suffer alternative consequences by going to jail to serve serious time. Therefore, no one reported him. I'm

sure cops on the Highland Park police department knew all about his actions but didn't give a damn.

Just when I was beginning to think *Officer Jackson's* actions of abuse were sort of a *Big Foot* myth, *Old Man* was put in the hospital. He'd gotten severely beaten, his drugs taken, but faced no charges and didn't go to jail. And just like the others, he never told police who the culprit was. He was now a victim of *Officer Jackson* (the rogue street cop, who would become a victim of his own rage and greedA). **Big Foot** was real, but he didn't stop our hustle.

On any given day, there were about ten of us holding down certain areas, and we were all looking out for Five-O (narcotic officers). Any narcotics car could be *Officer Jackson*. If someone yelled, **"Five-O,"** everyone would haul ass. We had our routes already mapped out if Five-O were spotted. It was always the same route.

The three incidents that changed the trajectory of my heroin hustle:

Incident One: On one fateful day, as we fled from Five-O and followed our route, an old homeowner had had enough of us running through his backyard and took aim with a .22 caliber rifle. I don't know if *Terry* was in his crosshairs when the man pulled the trigger or if he'd just aimed at the herd, hoping to hit someone, but he hit Terry in the back - dead center of his spine.

Terry went down immediately. We all hid on the other side of the fence, trying to decide who would go and help *Terry*. A short time later, EMS and police sirens could be heard. Those of us with drugs in our possession left the scene. The rest of us watched as EMS arrived and took *Terry* away. He never walked again.

Highland Park streets were cruel. *Terry's* shooting was the first real tragedy and a sort of reality check for us. Up until that point, the hustle was fun, and life was still a distorted fairy tale.

Born in California and transplanted here was a huge move, but not a monumental cultural shock. There were hustlers there, too, but I was too young to remember. Hell, the only thing I truly remember about California was the drive to Michigan. And now, here I was in Highland Park, hustling my ass off and jockeying for territory to beat out the competitors.

We were in disbelief when *Terry* went down. We contemplated revenge against the old man who shot him, but we didn't want the extra heat for his death. After all, we still had a business to run and didn't want a homicide to break up the team or shut down the operation altogether.

So, we gathered and shot up the man's house two nights later to frighten him. No homicides were reported that day, so apparently, he wasn't hit, but he had a hell of a lot of cleaning up to do the next morning. Maybe he would think twice before shooting, the next time we needed to use his yard as our getaway route. Nonetheless, Terry was done, and we couldn't change that. His hustle stopped right where he went down in that yard.

Following *Terry's* tragedy, his younger brother, *Kirk*, was cruel to *Terry*. P ri or t o be ing paraly ze d , *Terry* always exacted his authority over *Kirk* and slapped him around when he talked back. *Kirk* was always embarrassed because *Terry* did it in front of all of us.

Well, young *Kirk* would now get his revenge on *Terry* over the next few years. *Kirk* would get mad at *Terry* and tip his wheelchair over, then run. *Terry* started keeping a .38 revolver in his lap.

I don't know if he ever shot *Kirk* or not. It would not have surprised me if he had. *Terry* died about eight years later. His death may have had more to do with depression than his paralysis.

23

CHAPTER VI –
DELIVERING THE HARD STUFF

I always had my cousin deliver the goods to our drug spots. I never really hung around our spots and rarely witnessed anyone doing the drugs. But there was always something going on around those spots to liven them up. The guys sometimes had neighborhood girls there, or they would have poker parties for entertainment.

The team didn't think I was weak or anything for not hanging out at the parties too long. They simply thought I was above sitting around dope spots and wanted me to focus on supplying the goods. They were always willing to step in and do the necessary legwork, so I let them party, occasionally without interfering. They were eager to prove their worth, earn money, and have fun doing it.

I saw my cousin servicing a guy and I watched from the car. I thought I recognized this drug fiend purchasing a blow of *"Blue Magic."* Turns out, I did recognize the guy. This was the same guy who robbed me on the bus for a thirty-dollar bag of weed a year or so earlier.

He was an older guy in his mid-thirties and must have smelled weed on me as I sat on that bus because he, out of the blue, asked me if I would sell him some weed. I didn't want to sell my only bag of weed at the time but thought I'd sell it to him since I had it and he wanted it. He then asked me if he could see it before he purchased it. I took it out, and he smelled it. He timed it perfectly. As the bus came to a stop to pick up a passenger, this guy ran off the bus with my weed. I chased him to the door, but as he ran off, he suddenly stopped and turned around to face me. He then gestured with his hand in his pocket as if he had a gun. I held the door open so the bus wouldn't leave. I contemplated getting off, but didn't have a gun and decided not to. I hoped to see him again.

The son of a bitch got away with my weed, I thought to myself. It's a small world. Although I had never met him before, I certainly would see him again and would surely recognize him when I did.

And this was the time and place that I saw him again. I clearly had the upper hand.

I got out of the car and interrupted this transaction for the opportunity to positively identify this guy. My cousin thought it odd that I came over during this transaction, but I had to know for sure if this was him. I asked him to raise his head and look at me. He hesitated but did. Now, I was certain that this was the guy who had taken my weed. I then asked him if he remembered me and he denied it. I called him a liar.

My cousin, Gordo, turned him around to face me and said, **"Just say the word, I'm gonna bash this fucker's head in ... Say it!"** he demanded.

Just then, another heroin fiend, Popeye, obviously familiar with what was going on and knew *Gordo*, grabbed the bat and cracked the guy over the head. I grabbed the bat from him and said, ***"No, I'll take care of this... he's a customer."***

The fact was, I didn't want to see the guy get killed for a thirty-dollar bag of weed from a year or so ago. I couldn't live with that. So, I took his twenty dollars and made him go buy a pack elsewhere. As he walked away, I yelled, ***"I'm still $10 with you."*** I was simply saving face in front of my guys. I intervened because they wanted to set an example with this guy and were going to beat him to a pulp.

I looked closely at Popeye's arms and understood why they called him *Popeye*. He was given the street name *Popeye* because his arms were so big from heroin use that he grossly resembled *Popeye the Sailor Man* from the 70s cartoon.

I had no idea of the extent that heroin affected the human body until I looked at his forearms. They were so swollen that I did not believe they were real. They had no veins because he'd shot so much heroin into them that they disappeared. He had to find other locations on his body to shoot his heroin. I nearly broke down in tears just seeing him.

He was such a nice guy and was willing to do anything for me. I didn't just feel disgust looking at his arms riddled with track marks and no veins … but I felt disgust at the fact that I was providing him this shit. A sense of sorrow and pity overwhelmed me, but I kept my emotions hidden well.

Popeye needed a fix occasionally, and when I saw him, he never paid for another shot of heroin again. I advised my guys to give him a blow whenever he came around. I told them it was a payoff for keeping a lookout for the police. This was actually my perverted way of gifting him for continuously ruining his life.

These were the people I had the most influence over. They were willing to do anything to be a part of my world.

When I was away from the crew and reciting my prayers, I included *Popeye*. I shed a tear once or twice for him. Of course, he never knew how he impacted my life. But he had—and more than he ever knew.

Highland Park turned into a powder keg waiting to explode. There were different crews from everywhere, and occasionally you would hear about someone you knew who got shot or killed.

On a sunny afternoon, we decided to take a break and play ball. Back then, there were makeshift basketball courts right behind the garages where the rims were nailed up. We played basketball for hours. Fouls were common but not flagrant. But on this day, Crazy *DeAndre* (a cousin by marriage) committed a hard, unnecessary foul against a rival guy who hustled on the other side of town. This got serious really quickly. The guy left and swore to return to the spot in ten minutes. *Crazy DeAndre* urged me to take him to my sister's house to get my

Clint Eastwood's, *Dirty Harry* *.45* caliber revolver since it was closer.

Crazy Deandre was a real nutcase. He was *Black's* nephew, so I had to take him to get the gun. Otherwise, he would have told everyone I didn't give him a gun when he was threatened and needed it. He had so much bravado that he might have stayed there without a gun to prove he wasn't a punk. He was the type of guy who would put a bullet in the back of your head if you let him down … relative or not.

So, I obliged. I gave him the gun and prayed under my breath that the other guy hadn't returned. My prayers went unanswered - The guy was there waiting for *Crazy Deandre* and ready for a shootout.

They were faced off in the alley … Crazy *DeAndre* holding the .45 caliber downward but clearly visible. The other guy had a German Luger and what looked like a .38 caliber. He had both hands downward, but his guns were clearly visible as well. Both kept

repeating the phrase, *"What's **up**,"* while everyone else was hiding behind trees and garages during this five-minute Mexican standoff.

After about two minutes, I came from hiding, easing my way from behind the tree and creeping my way between them both, trying to defuse the situation.

I nervously argued how senseless this standoff was and that we should be playing ball. ***"This is not the reason for anyone to lose their life out here today,"*** I continued. ***"Let's just play ball."*** After about five minutes of convincing, the two went their separate ways. To this day, I'm shocked no one was killed during that standoff … mainly me!

A few years later, *Crazy DeAndre* came out of a family bar and was crossing Hamilton Avenue, on the same street where he lived. Someone walked up behind him and shot him point-blank in the back of the head.

Because no one ever wanted to confront *Crazy DeAndre*, I guess they killed him the only way they knew how – they surprised him with a blow to the back of the head. He never saw it coming.

Not much had changed over the course of time. We ran the streets, increased our drug trade, and hit the local gambling parties.

I made a few more friends over the years. They were the type that always expressed how they had my back. They always tried to assure me of what they would do for me. That was always a claim by the new guys, but *Rico* meant it.

Rico always wanted to go to yard parties in the neighborhood. I was never comfortable attending these types of parties. Since I was becoming more popular and wore gold chains, I knew I could be a potential target at those gatherings.

If you wore gold chains at those types of gatherings and a fight broke out, you had to be careful. Because if you weren't the intended target, you would quickly become the target. Thieves relished the opportunity to snatch gold chains in unruly crowds. However, because I had turned down so many of *Rico's* requests to attend the yard parties, I decided to go to one that night.

I usually carried a gun at these types of events, but I knew the consequences of getting caught with a pistol, so I had *Rico* carry his. Besides, he wanted to impress me and got his chance this night. He swore that nothing would happen to me. So, he loaded up and we went to the party.

Sure enough, a huge fight broke out. *Rico* ushered me out of the yard, and about five guys followed us. He threatened to kill them if they followed us any further. They shot in the air, so *Rico* laughed and let off four or five rapid shots in the air in their direction. His shots were much louder, so the guys immediately turned around and stopped following us.

Rico had proven his commitment to the team. He loved me like a brother. He constantly expressed his loyalty by always being there when I needed him. He was now a real team member and was cut in on a larger piece of the pie.

Over the next year or two, he proved that he was totally comfortable with me and I with him. He shared his upbringing and how his father beat the hell out of his mother. He also shared the story of how he lost his older brother to gun violence years earlier. I understood what he'd gone through and was even more honored to be a big brother for him.

Incident Two: Rico shared a story that I wish he hadn't. He mentioned that he rode his bike to the park one day to smoke some weed. He said two guys walked up attempting to rob him.

He, without hesitation, pulled out a gun and shot one of the guys in the head, killing him. He then took the guy's gun and his jewelry and fled. This story reminded me of an incident that happened to a kid that I had known - a kid that I remembered running to his mom's house to see him when she brought him home from the hospital as a newborn. I later found out that this was the kid that *Rico* killed. I was torn and didn't know how to react.

He wondered why my demeanor had suddenly changed towards him the next few days. I contemplated exposing his secret to the dead guy's brothers, but I knew he'd be dead by the end of the week. I simply pulled my support and cut ties with *Rico*. Luckily, I still had *Tim*, who was my cousin and was always eager to protect me as well. I never heard from *Rico* again. I hope he survived.

Incident Three: After dismissing *Rico*, *Tim* became the guy. He was my cousin, and I spent family reunions, funerals, weddings, and other family gatherings with him since childhood. He was now my ride-or-die guy.

Tim was just a few months older than me. He became my eyes and ears. I trusted him with my life. Although it never came to that, he was always ready and willing to be there if anything did go down. And I never doubted his willingness to protect me for a second. After a year, *Tim* got the hang of it and was making more money as well.

One morning, when we got to our spot for our morning rendezvous, there was a crazy buzz going around. There was a rumor that *Officer Jackson* was dead. We didn't believe it. I don't think anyone wished him dead but wanted him caught.

We always laughed about the thought of him getting busted and locked up with the same guys he had beaten and taken drug money from. We relished the day he would face lockup. But it appeared that someone was out for street justice. And if this was true, he certainly got what was coming to him - karma would have come full circle.

Turns out it was true. *Officer Jackson* was found in the same alley where he beat and robbed drug dealers. He was found beaten and had multiple needles protruding from his forearms. I think his official cause of death was an overdose.

Our primary problem was gone. Then suddenly, there was another issue lurking around the corner that hit me like a ton of bricks.

Tim, out of the blue, decided he was going to the Army. I think *Officer Jackson's* death scared the hell out of him. No one knew who did it or how other cops were going to retaliate or react to our hustle, but *Tim* was out.

Tim's departure felt like a gut punch. He was my *Rock of Gibraltar*. He was a vital part of my hustle, and my success depended on him. He had become my partner who made this lifestyle tolerable, and now he was gone!

CHAPTER VII –
THE ALTERNATIVE GAME

Things were changing. Suddenly, there was a seismic shift in the game. A different type of drug was introduced and fetched a tenfold profit compared to heroin. You mix cocaine with a third of baking soda in a heated bottle or pot—twirl it while it is heated, then take it away from the heat while continuing the slow twirl angled at 20 to 40 degrees. Suddenly, you held a valuable gem … crack cocaine. It was the wave of the future and seemed to expedite the hustle and everything that came with it.

Unfortunately, it sped up death, incarceration, abuse, and violence. With this new hustle and without *Tim* by my side, it was like looking at the world through a fishbowl … everything moved so fast that things became blurry.

At times, things were moving too fast-paced that I felt like I was living life through an outer body experience. I had to forcefully set aside my conscience to wholeheartedly indulge in this crack-hustle process, but it was hard—*Tim* was gone.

I never really cared much about the profit. I looked forward to simply rewarding the guys who had sacrificed for me. I wanted to keep my team happy and employed. This type of hustle was what they wanted to do. In a sense, I was throwing my life away trying to satisfy them. However, in the back of my mind, I had been subconsciously contemplating my exit, even before *Tim's* departure. I'd outgrown this game about six months into it but stayed loyal to it and to my friends anyway.

Turns out my new brother-in-law was truly one of the area's drug kingpins, and *Old Man* was his guy. I didn't like *Black* from the start.

31

I didn't know him, but I'd heard of him and knew of his reputation. As little (in stature) as he was, he was feared. I refused to deal directly with him.

I only wanted to deal with *Old Man*. Besides, he was my brother, and I was not trying to compete with him. I only wanted to recoup my drugs from him and be there to watch his back. The cocaine business was too fast-paced and treacherous for me not to be there for him if something went wrong.

This game drew very clever criminals. I thought *Old Man* would need me now more than ever before. But it wasn't the case. He handled this game with ease, and before I knew it, he was buying houses and fancy cars.

Although *Black* was financially loaded and bought my sister fancy cars and an extravagant house, I thought he was very disrespectful to her. He had girlfriends in different neighborhoods. My sister had always been so independent. She'd been on her own since high school. At age eighteen, she'd worked at a salon and had her own apartment.

At age twenty-three, she owned her own salon and house. She did not need this guy, and I knew it. But after a while, it became clear that she had become addicted to the lifestyle.

And now they were married. He was buying her Jaguars, minks, and all the other perks to keep a boss lady content. So, I accepted him but thought, one day my overprotective ass would have to come to her rescue. I had surprisingly grown taller than all my other brothers and was extremely protective of my sisters.

I was hoping my size would be an intimidation factor to this guy and would deter him from ever physically abusing my sister. He probably would have had me killed, but I didn't play when it came to my sisters and would've taken my chances. This guy surrounded us with a whole different breed of characters. I was now associating with known killers, gangsters, and wannabe gangsters. Hell—I was becoming one.

True to form, *Black* and I butted heads about his aggressiveness toward my sister while she was pregnant. He was a scumbag, and I had known it all along.

But we were family now. My brothers always had my back, regardless of the situation. *Steve* had just come home from Jackson Penitentiary after nearly twenty-seven years. He would certainly get involved, but I did not want him to go back to prison, so I tight-roped the situation and resisted the urge to directly confront *Black*.

I was fearless as well (or stupid) when it came to my sisters. I seemed to be constantly running to their rescue regarding issues between them and their boyfriends or husbands. It was so stupid of me. One of my sisters got into a fight with her husband. They always

fought. So, I asked her if I could stay with her for a couple of days. I was hoping this guy would come over while she wasn't there. But he never did.

He would see my car in the driveway and wouldn't come into the house. So, one day I parked two blocks over and hid in the house. Sure enough, he came in with her. I could hear her searching closets and behind sofas for me. When she was certain I wasn't in the house, she called him in from the car I was hidden in a small closet underneath some coats.

When he came in, I tried to cut the door exit off from him, but my sister barricaded the closet door and he made it out of the house and into his car. I ran after him with a .223 caliber rifle. I wasn't going to shoot but demanded he get out of the car. As I reached for the passenger door to get him out, he hit the locks. I was running around the car to reach the driver's side door, where he was curling up in fear, when my sister jumped on my back, and I fell onto the walkway, dropping the gun. The gun hit the sidewalk and slid down the driveway. He saw this and immediately jumped out of the car, grabbed the gun, and was now pointing it at me and threatening to shoot.

My sister begged him not to shoot. He was a military guy and looked at the gun. He knew exactly what it was. He left with the gun and came back with the police. They began questioning me about the gun. I told them to arrest him. I informed them that he had pulled the gun on me. I dodged a bullet but lost that gun. Fortunately, neither of us went to jail

I became the poster boy for protecting the women in my family. I had aunties and cousins calling about their boyfriends raising their hands and voices to them. It became embarrassing to me—and it became even more embarrassing that they always returned to the very same guys I had confronted. It was pathetic.

My mother once had a policewoman friend who played Gin Rummy with a group of other women. This woman knew about my reputation and called to tell me that my mother's boyfriend had hit my mother. I was so outraged that I didn't listen to the rest of the story or think to myself that this woman was a cop and could have simply subdued this guy or called for backup. Why didn't she handle it? I questioned these things internally, but knew I had to get there anyway – and fast. I called several people (even a taxi). But no one showed up fast enough. It was

only a mile away, and I could not wait any longer. I grabbed a *Louisville Slugger* and ran out the door.

I had to get there as fast as I could. After all, the woman cop who called me had known Mom for years—she would not exaggerate this. Maybe she didn't want to shoot him or take him to jail. Everything was going through my mind. Maybe she wanted to see him get his ass kicked. I don't know what her reasoning was, but I was on my way to do just that.

I rushed to get there before he left—and wouldn't you know it. As I reached the block, there he was walking down the street, eyes bucked as if he'd just whooped my mom's ass and was leaving the scene.

I ran him down and began swinging like *Joe DiMaggio*... I pounded this poor guy... teeth were flying everywhere. People peered through their front doors but stayed only spectators. Suddenly, a woman came from nowhere, approaching me in a hesitant manner, but staying at bay. I immediately stopped and looked at her. She froze in her tracks as if she'd realized, at that moment, that she could be a victim too.

In a tone of empathy, she asked me why I wanted to kill this guy. I said he hit my mother. The woman said, "Oh," and walked away. But her empathy made me realize that he'd had enough. I continue to run the remaining half-block to check on my mother.

When I got there, she was coming out of the bathroom. I asked her if she was alright. She nonchalantly said she was fine as if nothing ever happened. I was a little puzzled by her response. She wasn't worked up, bruised, nor did she let out a sigh of relief to see me.

She looked at me. You could see her expression change as she examined my being. She suddenly let out a slow, silent gasp and, under her breath, asked if I'd hurt him. I explained the phone call and that I caught him trying to get away. She almost cried before she turned her attention to the cop. She was fuming. Her blood pressure was already high—it must have gone through the roof at that moment.

This guy never put his hands on her. I didn't see any bruises, and no one was acting as if anything had happened. She looked at me in disbelief and said, **"Boy, you know that man didn't put his hands**

on me." She continued, **"I would've put that knife in his butt."** I knew she would have.

I was flabbergasted that nothing actually happened. I asked if she was sure. She assured me again, but this time with an air of amazement as if I knew better than to think that he would have hit her.

I then told her what I had just done. She exclaimed, **"No, you** *didn't!"* Then ran out the door looking for him. I was devastated and too embarrassed to help in the search. I wanted to kill the cop woman. She knew how overprotective I was, and I was certain she didn't like the guy. But I never questioned her credibility or her intentions, so I became the pawn in her plan.

I had done this for every one of my sisters. It got so bad that I was getting calls from more of my women relatives complaining about their boyfriends (some I hadn't talked to in years) - enough was enough. There was enough envy and revenge in these mean streets to dodge. I didn't need these unnecessary family challenges. Every relationship that I've ever intervened on behalf of my sisters was for not ... They were back with the guys within a week. I was losing my focus. My mission was to strengthen my bond with my team and keep the money rolling in, not to play "Captain-Save-A-Ho" with these women.

My mother and sisters forgave me. However, I intervened more than once with two of them. I don't think any of them, save my mother, even considered the potential repercussions of their actions to purposely involve me. I don't blame them, though. I blame myself for my blind love for them. I should have been more careful and less involved in their relationships.

I did learn a valuable lesson along the way: I learned that you can't choose who your siblings love, but you can, and should determine your level of involvement in their affairs.

CHAPTER VIII –
MY CELEBRITY ENCOUNTER

I never thought much about Florida. My buddies tried to convince me for years that it was the ultimate tourist destination and that we should go. I personally felt that if I never visited the Sunshine State, I wouldn't have missed much. I had no aspirations of ever going there. But oddly enough, I found myself going to Miami quite often. My sister and brother-in-law owned a house there and had listed it on the market. Occasionally, I convinced them to let me go and check on it.

I made excuses to go down there and had some very memorable times. There were three trips to Miami that I will never forget. I don't regret them, but they weren't great. The first incident, in which I never thought I would leave a free man, wasn't even drug-related.

On *my first trip*, my girlfriend and I, along with another couple, had spent five fun-filled days in Miami. Before we left, we decided to visit a few restaurants for breakfast on the day of our departure. We headed down Ocean Drive looking for a good breakfast spot. We found one, and the food was great. I remember sitting next to the actor Bruce Willis. He was nice. He smiled and chatted with us as we ate.

After breakfast, we stopped at Fat Tuesday and drank delicious slushes. There must've been hundreds of flavors in twirling cylinders along the walls. Every flavor must have contained twenty percent alcohol or even more. But as we drank them, we hadn't noticed the potency. The drinks went down so smoothly. We must have knocked back two or three apiece - the buzz snuck up on us. We were so toasted when we left the restaurant that I didn't realize I left my credit card until we were blocks away. We ran back, and the hostess was holding it at the door. She was sweet so I tipped her. We decided to stroll down Ocean Drive once more before our departure.

As we continued our walk, my girlfriend exclaimed, "There's **Naomi Campbell**!" We looked, and there was a crowd of beautiful models walking away from this house. We never doubted that it was Naomi Campbell, because we learned the house belonged to *Gianni Versace*. It was amazing how this single house sat alongside all these restaurants on Ocean Drive.

There was restaurant, restaurant, restaurant ... then Gianni Versace's house ... then more restaurants. His house stood out like a sore thumb, and the women came from that direction.

We were so excited and tipsy that we stopped and took pictures of the house. That's when I proposed a crazy idea. I would jump the fence, put my hand near the doorknob, and have my girlfriend take a picture before I jumped back out. I would jump in and out before anyone would notice. They couldn't believe it, but I did it. It was a success. Even though they stalled me to get more pictures, we got them before anyone came in or left the house.

Hours later, when we got to the airport, there was breaking news. *Gianni Versace* had just been shot and killed just outside his home. Someone had laid in ambush when he returned to the house from eating lunch. I was mortified. I liked *Versace*, but sympathy took a back seat to my fears. I had just jumped his fence and taken pictures at his front door.

I was certain that there was no way I was going to board that plane without being arrested. There had to be a video camera somewhere in that yard showing me jump that fence. My heart was beating a mile a minute. The breaking news was on every monitor at the airport.

I made my friends delete all the pictures they had of me on from their phones on that estate. I knew I was going to be detained, at least until I could prove my innocence. We boarded the plane without incident. But then, I expected to be extradited as soon as we landed. I assumed their investigation was at least that far ahead.

By the time we landed back in Michigan, it had been reported that the police had a person of interest. I thought it was me. It was later revealed that the person was someone named *Andrew Cunanan*. Turns out, he'd murdered a few other people, then killed himself. I was glad they found him.

My second trip to Miami was under the guise of moving furniture from Florida back to Michigan. My brother-in-law and my sister offered to pay me to clear out their house when they sold it. I would be paid handsomely to transport the furniture back to Michigan. I decided to take a break from the hustle and take my buddies up on their desire to get away. It was my brother-in-law's request that I recruit my friends to help with the task. Of course, we could stay a few extra days at the house. It was sort of like an Airbnb vacation situation.

32

Suddenly, here I was, following *Black* and headed to Florida again. I was headed south again. Now i was visiting Florida more often than I'd ever imagined. When we got there, *Black* shared his true intention with me, secretly. He didn't share this with my team but only me. There was a secret compartment on the van's passenger entrance step. It opened, and there were two kilos of cocaine hidden in the compartment area.

I was offered five thousand dollars to get it back to Detroit. I was asked not to mention this to my team. This clandestine offer was no challenge to my loyalty to my team. They always had my back, and now I had theirs. I informed *Black* that there was no way I was getting on the highway transporting two keys without my team knowing the true nature of this mission. I promised him I would negotiate a fair price with the guys and get it done.

There were five of us and two trucks: the U-Haul and the van. I presented the situation to the guys in the form of an ultimatum. They could get fifteen hundred dollars apiece to transport two kilos while we brought the furniture back to the D, or we could tell him to *"Go to Hell."* I told them fifteen hundred dollars was a fair price if they decided to do it. They didn't hesitate and agreed. We made the trek without a hitch.

Four of those idiots accepted an eighth of a key as payment. By the time they morphed it into crack they realized that shit was stepped on so badly with baking soda and other additives that it was the equivalent of an 8-ball when they finished cooking it.. They complained to me, but there was nothing I could do. They should have accepted the cash.

I learned a lot about *Black* after that trip and never wanted to deal with him again. He was a treacherous dealer who was extremely streetwise and feared. And, at that point, he was also one of the more profitable dealers in Detroit. He was supplying half the city. It's no wonder he was so paid. He and my sister were rubbing shoulders with quite a few celebrities.

My third trip to Miami was when I accompanied *Black* and two of his buddies on a trip to Miami. We were there to promote some underwear. Walt wanted to meet with some of the designers to pitch some snakeskin, Velcro-latching underwear. I look back at that

moment and think that that had to be one of the dumbest fuckin' ideas I'd ever heard. I gave him an *A* for effort, though and we were all in.

We had about six thousand dollars between the four of us for the three-day trip. We gambled every night, and there was a different winner between us every night. Every one of our inner characters seemed to emerge when we won. *Black's* actions during and after that trip surprised me more than I could have imagined.

While we gambled, each winner treated the others to dinner that night, then breakfast in the morning. When *Black* won, he would always instigate an argument with his buddy, *Eddie*. I could sense that they weren't the best of friends, and lingering tensions surfaced at times between the two.

During that trip, Eddie took a liking to me and even offered me a job when we got back to Michigan. He swore I'd make more money than I'd ever seen in my life. I was looking forward to seeing what he had to say. I couldn't wait to get back to Michigan.

Turns out, he was the only heroin dealer among us and was a huge figure in the heroin game back home and he made a lot of money. I wondered if that was the reason Black exhibited so much animosity toward Eddie during our trip.

One week after returning to Detroit, Eddie was killed—shot in the back over a gambling dispute while playing pool at his house. I was told there were three guys in his basement playing pool when it happened. *Black* was one of them - There went my chances of any opportunity to make *more money than I'd ever seen*. The triggerman was never identified.

CHAPTER IX –
THE FALLOUTS

*O*ld Man had a falling out with *Black* not long after *Eddie* was killed. I never knew what triggered their fallout. Following that fallout, my brother had somehow broken both his legs. *Old Man* told me he was with a girl and had to jump from a second-story window to flee from her jealous boyfriend, who forced his way into *her* apartment. I never believed that story, but I went with it.

He secured a new connect. He made a serious connection and started moving mounds of kilos of cocaine. Because of his new connection, I overstayed my welcome in the drug game. Funny thing is his new connect was Ace Man—the same guy who pulled up on me crying when **Rockin' Rod** was killed. My focus was to be there to protect him and, of course, earn a little money along the way. He had a lot of people around him sucking up to be in his inner circle, and that always concerned me about him.

Old Man eventually supplied me with heavy weight to push. I received as many kilos as I could move. But oddly enough, he never wanted me hanging out with him and his friends. I thought maybe he was shielding me from the streets, but that didn't make sense—after all, he provided me with all this cocaine, and it was his lead I was following!

Nevertheless, my teams were holding it down at my spots. I had one spot where all my friends loved to hang out. The girls across the street liked me and stopped by whenever they saw my car outside. I even dated one of them briefly. They were cool and loved to stop by and have a drink or just sit and chat when I visited.

I occasionally visit my spots to check on sales and collect money.

The guys who rode with me would often ask me if they could stay and keep an eye on this spot (sort of hold it down for me). I wanted to make sure that the guy who lived there wasn't double-dipping and dealing for my competitors as well. So sometimes, I let them stay. However, I think their true intentions were to get closer to the girls across the street.

Previously, the homeowner accepted my weekly fee but was dealing someone else's dope on the premises. I was pissed and roughed him up a bit for sharing the spot with multiple rivals. This was the kind of

greed that usually got someone killed. It always caused unnecessary problems.

I was headed there, on what turned out to be a very eventful day, with my best friend, *Roby;* my friend *Rockin' Rod*, who was a professional boxer and had no business running with us; and my lame-ass uncle, *Tall T*. He and *Rockin' Rod* were just dying to hang out at the spot.

Tall T was my mother's youngest brother. He was hoping to get lucky with one of the girls across the street. But that wasn't happening. *Uncle Tomboy (his brother)* was head of homicide. There was no way I was going to leave *Tall T* at that house and have something go wrong. I did not want to answer to *Uncle Tomboy* about his little brother getting caught in a drug raid or worse.

This was *Roby's* designated spot, so he had every intention of staying there. We were simply dropping him off. He usually stayed there and ran things anyway. *Rockin' Rod* had never been there but saw the girls on their porch. So, he decided to stay with *Robe* until I returned.

The three girls from across the street were always an incentive for everyone to hang out at my spot. After we arrived, the girls came over as if on cue. But today was about business. I couldn't have them sitting around while I reprimanded the homeowner about what I was hearing. I asked them to leave and advised them to come back in an hour or so and we could all hang out and have drinks.

I scolded the homeowner and reminded him about violating our deal. He admitted his actions and apologized for them. I'd suddenly lost all trust and respect I had for this guy. When it was time to leave, *Rockin' Rod* and *Tall T* asked me if they could stay. I told them no, but they implored, and I gave in, so *Rockin' Rod* stayed. I wished he hadn't!

I told him I'd be back in an hour to pick him up. I told *Tall T*, who was looking for a free high and some free pussy, that under no circumstances could he stay. He was my youngest uncle—my mother's baby brother. And *Uncle Tomboy* was head of Narcotics out of Thirteen Hundred Beaubien at the time. How ironic was that? So, it was a hard no for *Tall T*.

I literally made him come with me. H*e* was not staying at that drug house. I would not be responsible nor to blame if that house got raided or, God forbid, something else happened. The last thing I needed was for *Uncle Tomboy* to be in my face blaming me for that grown man's dumb-ass decision to chill in a dope house. So, we left. But as we walked out, both guys, *Rockin' Rod* and *Roby* asked me to stop by their moms' houses to get a change of clothes for them. I thought it odd but agreed to do it since neither was too far out of the way.

I stopped at *Roby's* mom's first and told her that he needed a change of clothes. After about five minutes, she handed me his clothes but gave me a concerned look and asked if he was okay. I assured her he was, then left.

Rockin' Rod's mom's house was next. I was sure his brother would answer the door, but it was his mom who came to the door. I explained that *Rockin' Rod* needed a change of clothes. She asked where he was and, with an air of concern, asked if he was okay? I said he was at his girlfriend's house and assured her he was fine.

The ride back was weird. *Tall T* and I were thinking the same thing. Both of their moms asked me if they were okay. That was weighing on me for some strange reason. We puffed a joint, set the thought aside, and headed back to the spot with their clothes.

As we pulled onto the block, there were police cars everywhere. And even a coroner. I could see someone who looked like my brother *Beast Boy* throwing cops aside, trying to make his way into the house. As we glanced from a distance at all the lights and activity, my phone rang. It was one of the girls from across the street.

She advised me that everyone in the house was dead. She watched the coroner pull *Roby's* and *Rockin' Rod's* bodies from the house. I drove by in disbelief—I was sick to my stomach.

After an hour or so, my phone rang. It was *Uncle Tomboy* . He wanted to meet me at my grandma's house immediately. *Tall T* begged me to drop him off somewhere else. He wanted no part of this shit. I looked at him as if he was deranged. I was the last person seen walking out of a drug house where everyone was killed, and he was my only witness. I assured him that he was going with me and nowhere else.

CHAPTER X –
THE INTERROGATION

When I got to my grandmother's house, *Uncle Tomboy* asked *Tall T* to wait upstairs. Then he led me to the basement and channeled his *Columbo* character. I'm sure the lights were intentionally left off except for the lamp in the middle of the table for the full effect of a police interrogation room. I was being interrogated right there in my grandma's basement. I have to say, it was better than meeting him downtown. I hated the dingy police headquarters. I had been there a couple of times and didn't want to go back. Regardless, I was the last one at that house and the last one to see everyone alive. So, since I had to be questioned here—it was better here than at police headquarters.

My only defensive strategy was my witness, *Uncle Tom's* pinch-hitting younger brother, *Tall T*. He was by my side the entire time. He never left my passenger seat. So whatever *Uncle Tomboy* was willing to do to me, his baby brother would face the same fate. I was worried, but I had my alibi locked tight.

When it was over, I went home. I had to collect my thoughts. I had just lost two friends and couldn't fathom what had just happened two hours prior. It became too much to process. I knew someone had to pay, but with everyone dead, I didn't know where to start or who to blame. Although I got through that interrogation, I knew it was just a matter of time before I would be hauled downtown and questioned again. It was inevitable.

The head of homicide was my uncle, but I was certain he was going to have another one of his cop cronies handle the next round of questioning. And this time, it would be tougher. But I was resting on my alibi and hoping they would find out who went in there and killed everybody.

Suddenly, my phone rang. I looked at the number and realized it was *Uncle Tomboy* again. I didn't want to answer. I knew he would ask me to come to the station this time. And that was too close to lockup. I wasn't prepared to be locked up—not even for a day. I ignored the call. I was doing my own investigation. I called the girls and asked them

if they saw anyone go into that house when I left. They told me they saw a car pull up. But before I could follow up, *Uncle Tomboy* was ringing in again. I advised the girls that I would call them back.

I worked up the courage to answer the call. *Uncle Tomboy* called to tell me that the homeowner, shot in the head and chest, pulled through surgery. He then asked me if I wanted to admit anything before this guy was questioned. I admitted that I had roughed him up a little for instigating trouble, but I had nothing else to admit.

All the while, I thought, Holy Shit—a witness. And he'll live to testify. Fate seemed to be on my side. This guy was so high off freebasing that he survived an execution-style attack. He was shot, point blank, in the head and chest with a 9mm caliber. It was amazing he pulled through. There would be no vigilante justice. This guy was definitely going to identify who shot him and killed *Roby* and *Rockin' Rod*. I was off the hook, but the perps were going to spend the rest of their lives in jail.

I was elated about being let off the hook. But I didn't know what amazed me more; him making it through to testify, or the fact that this guy was so high on cocaine it actually saved his life and, in turn, possibly saved mine. The exhilaration was short-lived. I suddenly realized that I was never going to see my friends again, and it hurt.

Two days later, the police had their suspects.

CHAPTER XI –
THE SUSPECT & THE VICTIM

Four years prior to the homicide, I left the heroin game for the cocaine game and took my talents to the west side of Detroit. I got a flat on Greenfield Road near Pembroke Street with two of my partners. We were going to change the game. We went to the same high school. *Roby* and I lived on the same block—across the street from one another. *Horse Boy* lived two blocks over.

This flat would be our stash house. We would store our drugs and guns there. It was agreed that one of us would be there overnight on any given night so that there was always someone in the house. We usually rotated our turns. We had grown really close through the years. That's why, years later, it shocked the hell out of me that it was *Horse Boy* who was convicted of entering my spot and killing *Robe* and *Rockin' Rod*. He apparently watched the house and waited until I left before entering the spot with his cousin and attempting to kill everyone in the house.

Rockin' Rod boxed for Ace Promotions. This boxing promotion game was one of *Ace Man's* multiple business ventures. He owned funeral homes, stores, and even had a small share in one of the major airlines. I later heard he also had other businesses. Unfortunately, he never completely left the game. But I did learn that *Rockin' Rod* was like a son to him. So, I had to find him and break the news of *Rockin' Rod's* death to him. Only I didn't know him and didn't know how to reach him.

It was coincidental how I got his phone number and was able to call him on his boat. This was my chance to tell him about *Rockin' Rod's* sudden death. I knew he was once (if not still) one of the biggest drug pushers in Detroit—at least one of the most financially successful ones. I was terrified that I had to be the one to break the news to him. But I had to advise him for my own protection.

About a year earlier, I met a girl named *Vicky* at the Budweiser Superfest concert. I had a cousin who sang for the Spinners, and his daughter *Che Che* would always have backstage passes for me if I wanted them. I met Vicky there and let her and a friend go backstage. I really connected

with her from that point on, and we started dating. We became inseparable after that concert.

Vicky was the first girl that I contemplated getting out of the game for. She was college-bound and very beautiful. She got pregnant about six months into the relationship and never told me. It was her mom who broke the news to me. She begged me to convince *Vicky* to have an abortion. *Vicky* had just graduated from high school and her mom had plans for her to go away to college. She pleaded that I convince *Vicky* not to be a mother at this time and promised me that, if our relationship was meant to be, it would happen when *Vicky* was more established. She also advised me that we would have plenty of time to get married and have kids in the future.

I thought to myself, there was no way I was going to convince this girl to have an abortion for me. I really didn't want her to. But then I considered her mom, who was practically begging me to help steer this girl back on track. It was the hardest thing I ever had to do. I convinced her that we could do it again after she graduated and became more settled. I told her that I would fully support her and would always be there. I sat with her and listened to her cry every night that I was there. This was so painful that I decided from that moment on, I would never have kids out of wedlock. I was devastated that I was a part of this shit.

I visited *Vicky* nearly every day for weeks. We never left her house for about two months straight. I never told her that I didn't believe in abortions or that her mom put me up to it.

When she went through with the abortion, her mom thanked me in a private whisper. I wanted to say, *fuck you*, but I had too much respect for her ambition to send her daughter off to college.

Vicky resented me afterward and left for college. We reconnected years later, but things were different. We'd lost whatever it was that we had. She wanted to spend the night, but I thought of all the things that her mother had gone through to keep this woman on track. She was still gorgeous, but the desire wasn't there anymore. I thought about what we lost, and I was too deflated to take advantage of her. She wanted it, but I just couldn't.

It turns out, *Vicky's* best friend was *Ace Man's* daughter. Ironically, she was the one with *Vicky* when I let her go backstage during the

Budweiser Superfest concert. That's how I got *Ace Man's* phone number to inform him of *Rockin' Rod's* death. When I called him and broke the news, it got quiet. I could hear him sobbing. He suddenly asked me where I was.

I was terrified. I told him that I was home and attempted to explain what had happened prior to giving him my address. I wanted to comfort him, because even though he didn't sound worked up, I knew he was upset. I tried to explain further, but he interrupted to ask for my address. I didn't have a choice. I gave him the address. Everything went through my mind. I assumed he would have someone come by and kill me. So, I called my brother and told him what I'd just done, but asked him not to come over. I did not want this to go wrong if *Ace Man's* plan was not to kill me. I wasn't going to create any more tension regarding the situation.

I sat on my porch and waited for about an hour. At first, a Porsche drove by, and the driver slowed in front of my house, staring at me as he cruised past. Then a Corvette did the exact same thing. Then came the long black Mercedes SEC 500. It parked right in front of my house. *Ace Man* stepped out -- crying. I didn't know whether to walk and meet him at the end of the walkway or not.

So, I just stood until he reached the porch then we sat. His eyes were tearing, and he couldn't stop sobbing. Through all the crying, he managed to ask me what happened.

Here I was explaining while he was bawling his eyes out. It was apparent that *Rockin' Rod* meant a lot to him. After I explained the situation, he got up, shook my hand, then thanked me and left. When he left, I remember feeling a little frightened. I was spared for now. But if there were going to be consequences, how would his revenge be exacted for *Rockin' Rod's* death?

I was spared that day. But about a week later, someone very close to my brother and I was murdered in the worst way possible.

Chris was my brother's number one guy, and I dated his sister for a while. When *Chris* didn't pick up his phone for either of them, I worried.

My brother told me *Chris* hadn't picked up for him in two days. I knew he hadn't picked up for his sister as well. He always answered his

phone for *Old Man*—but not this time. I knew immediately that something was wrong. I thought about my meeting with *Ace Man*. I wondered if *Chris's* death was revenge. Had he been crucified because of *Rockin' Rod's* death?

Chris turned up two days later, beaten to death, then shot twice and thrown into a neighborhood trash bin. This was overkill. The case was never solved. I hated to think that *Chris* was the sacrificial lamb for things that had gone wrong in the game, but this thought consumed me.

Ace Man had spared me. He was one of the most powerful neighborhood drug lords and I had escaped his rage. To all of us, he was untouchable. Out of reach from any petty crimes or revenge attempts. I could remember *Black* telling my brother that anyone could be gotten. I guess he was right.

Two years later, someone was killed outside the **Page One Club** on Seven Mile Road just one block east of the Southfield Service Drive. Turns out, it was *Ace Man*. He'd been shot more than fifty times while getting into the same black SEC 500 Mercedes Benz that he had pulled up in at my house following *Rockin' Rod's* death. I guess he was t-o-u-c-h-a-b-l-e.

These streets were mean, and when it came to competition and envy, everyone was touchable. *Black* met a younger woman and left my sister alone in a six-hundred-thousand-dollar home in West Bloomfield Hills. He moved into a house he bought for his mother on the west side of Detroit.

Black left his mother's house headed to his favorite spot: **Banko's Lounge** on Wyoming and Intervale Street. He never made it. As he attempted to exit his side door, someone was waiting in the dark and blew half his head off with a .45 caliber gun. My nephew was the only one there. He sat in the doorway crying, hugging what was left of his dead dad's head in his arms.

After everything *Black* did in these streets and with his reputation, he had moved back to the city. If anyone knew better, it should have been him. No one was safe from these treacherous streets or this game, especially him. But for some reason, he came back.

CHAPTER XII –
MY LEGAL WOES

Old Man had secured another connection. His new connection provided him with all the coke he needed. He was now a force to be reckoned with. He had his number one and number two guys, but my stock shot up as well. He was moving about 125 kilos a month and provided me with as many kilos as I could move. My ten-dollar boulders were so big that no one could compete. My method was quantity over profit. **Move it!** was my motto. I made enough money to play around, look the part, and keep my guys happy. That was enough for me. Besides, I had to impress *Old Man* to keep the stuff flowing in.

Part of the fun for me was watching his back and seeing him rise through the ranks. But, as much as I wanted to be there to protect him, *Old Man* never wanted me around his team. I never understood it. He was always willing to do anything to protect me and provided me with a lot of coke, so why didn't he want me around—that puzzled me.

Maybe it was because of the things I saw. For example, we gambled a lot, and I counted superfast. I was a silent street math whiz. No one could count faster than me or cheat me out of my money. I was the only one who could count faster than he could. When we gambled, I could always keep up with the bets and the money. I hadn't graduated high school, but I always counted and wrote very well. *Old Man* was so clever that he never changed the fifties nor hundred-dollar bills that hit the pavement during our dice games.

Old Man was so clever that he never changed the fifties nor hundred-dollar bills that hit the pavement during our dice games. He had a strategy. He never changed the big bills but always kept track of what was owed to him. I listened to him count into the guys' money and thought how his math was so bad that he would devour an entire hundred-dollar bill in ten minutes. I never said anything, but I insisted I get change before I played with anything larger than a twenty-dollar bill. That way, I'd keep the arguments down. Besides, I didn't want the guys to see me challenging and correcting his math. I was just hoping they followed my lead. There was no wonder why he always won and earned another nickname, *Lucky Goat*.

Besides his clandestine gambling habits, I loved the fact that he was always there when I needed him. I had some strange run-ins with some Young Boys Incorporated (YBI) members when I started getting a little money, and when I needed a way out, *Old Man* was Johnny-on-the-spot.

Ladies liked me, but I was never a ladies' man like *Old Man*. I could only date one girl at a time. He dated multiple hood queens simultaneously. He even went out with one of the girls from the singing group, En Vogue. I was impressed; I'd always liked those girls.

I didn't like drama and only dated girls who didn't draw a lot of attention. So, when I met *Angie*, I was stepping out of my comfort zone. Her appearance reminded me of one of *Old Man's* girls. She was funny, beautiful, and had an hourglass figure. She knew a lot of the local drug dealers. She wasn't my typical type, but I really wanted her— She dripped sexuality. Everything about her attracted me.

She invited me over to her house one night, and we did the business. I thought I was the luckiest dude alive lying there naked as she puffed her cigarette and exhaled perfect smoke rings.

But then, as I lay there entertained by her smoke ring talent, I heard loud and rapid knocks at the door. I thought, *Oh shit! She's got a man*. She assured me she didn't but then advised me to stay in the room and be very quiet. She told me that *Timmy P* owned the house and lived in the upstairs flat sometimes.

While she tried to calm me before answering the door, another round of knocks pierced our silence. I had heard about *Timmy P* and his guys for years. They called themselves YBI. They were getting a lot of money and were leaving trails of bodies of anyone who challenged them or got in their way. And now, here I was, trapped in a room in his house.

I could hear maybe three guys entering the flat. One of them asked her if she had company. She said in a low tone, **"He's nobody important."** She continued to chat with them, not in a quiet but a normal tone. At that time, I got no indication they were planning to leave anytime soon. I had a gun but knew I was outgunned. I didn't want a shootout with these guys anyway.

From the sound of things, I could tell she was being cautious and didn't sound anxious to get rid of them. So, I had to think fast.

I called *Old Man* and asked him (in a whispered tone) to come get me, and that I was in a little jam. Luckily, he was nearby. He happened to be taking care of some business in that neighborhood. He was there in five minutes. I left out the back porch door, ran around to the front of the house, hopped in the Corvette and we were out of there.

The other YBI incident was when I met *Kenny*. I met him while serving the longest jail stint of my life. I had a warrant for my arrest once, and the police came to my house to arrest me two years after an incident.

Two years earlier, I'd just come from Florida and saw a guy named *Coffee* who I rented a car from before I left. He was in front of a house with a few of his boys getting high when I turned the corner near Plymouth and Forrer roads. He saw me and flagged me down, so I stopped and had my buddy pay him for the rental we used a week prior. He handed the guy a twenty-dollar crack bag. I didn't even know he was carrying drugs.

I noticed narcotic officers were right behind us. We hadn't noticed them and had no idea where they came from. But I didn't stop until he jettisoned every bag he had on him out the window. I wasn't driving at a fast pace, but I was doing 25 mph on the residential street. I simply wanted to find a group of dope fiends in the area so he could throw it out in front of them, and hopefully, they'd pick it up. When he threw it out, I drove around for a few more blocks, providing ample time for the drugs to be devoured by the dope fiends who saw him throw it.

But when I stopped, one of the narcotic officers ushered us out of the car, patted us down, and then searched the vehicle. We had nothing. But just then, a cop came running around the corner with about seven packs of cocaine that my buddy had thrown out of the window. He apparently saw him throw them out of the window, then got out of the cop car, and picked up the packs where the cop saw my buddy throw them out.

And now, two years later, as I slept, I was awakened by a loud knock at the door on a Saturday morning. My sister and I were living together. I slept on the floor in my room and kept all my illegal guns on the waterbed. I hated that waterbed and had back problems every time I slept on it. I had

about twenty guns with no safe, so I kept them in the waterbed under a blanket.

It was about nine in the morning when they came. The knocks were so loud that I went to grab a gun to go answer the door. Before I could grab a gun and head to the door, my sister had already opened the door and let the cops in. One of them warned her to drop the knife. She was cutting potatoes for breakfast.

When I heard that, I threw the gun back on the bed in the room and walked out. I had on my pajama bottoms with no shirt. There were two officers in the house already. I watched the officer with a hand on his holstered gun by his side. As I came out of the room, he asked me if I was *Larry?* I confirmed, and he announced that he had a warrant for my arrest.

I told him I had to put some clothes on. I thought about all the cocaine residue on the scale that was on the other side of my bed. Most of all, I worried that he would see all those guns once I opened the door to my room. I was certain those would lead to a whole list of new charges. But as he walked toward me, I cracked the door and grabbed a sheet from the makeshift floor-bed near the door, made of folded blankets and sheets.

As I tossed the sheet in the air, I prayed he wouldn't see those guns. As the sheet came down over the bed, it opened completely (like a parachute) and lightly settled over the bed, covering all the guns. The officer stood in view of the room, but I stood as close to the door as possible to put my clothes on while attempting to block his view. I grabbed the shirt off the dresser near the door and put it on without fully opening the door. I saw the cop peeking around me for any remnants of a new crime. I guess you could say I was blessed that day because he never saw anything and didn't have a search warrant to search my room, only an arrest warrant.

I was in the backseat of a cruiser headed downtown. I would be detained for my longest jail stint ever … three whole days.

CHAPTER XIII –
TIME TO REFLECT

I was headed to the "old" county jail. That meant I had to go through a tunnel, and as claustrophobic as I am, I didn't think I'd make it to the other side alive. As I begged for oxygen, the cop assured me that we were almost there.

I made it. I didn't know how long I was to be subjected to these new surroundings, but it turned out to be three days. I'd been in local lockups for traffic violations before, but this was different. I had to put on a jumpsuit as if I were in prison. I adjusted as best I could. I had to make the best of a fucked-up situation.

Three days was plenty of time for me to think about how my life was spiraling off track. I reminisced about everything when I laid down. Was my father turning over in his grave? Were his last words to me; "Take Care," said in vain?

I didn't know if he was actually turning in his grave, but I was certain I wasn't living up to his last two words spoken to me on his deathbed. I promised I would, but this game had its claws in me, and I knew it too well.

A strange guy befriended me while in lockup. His name was *Kenny*. He bragged about his pink Mercedes Benz and all the women he attracted. He laughed about a gold chain he wore. He had a Run-

D.M.C. rope with a gold mirrored medallion. He shared a line with me that he used on girls.

He'd approach a girl and ask her to look at his charm. She'd look at his charm and see her reflection. Then he asked her, ***"Don't we look***

good together?"

He laughed about how well that line worked. I thought it was Pretty **fuckin' cheesy**. But I could see why it worked so well on women— it was a charming approach for this monster.

As we chatted while in lockup, he explained that he was a member of the YBI but had fallen on hard times. He mentioned that he was locked up for dealing drugs. I wondered if it was drug usage or drug selling.

We formed a bond, and he earned my trust. He had served five months of a six-month sentence there while I was serving three days. I promised him that when he got out, I would help him get back on his feet. I had a connection and could help him. I was a man of my word.

When he got out thirty days later, he called me. I supplied him with small packages. He always came up short, but he was trying. So, I only provided him with one half of an ounce at a time. While we were at his house weighing out his sack, he showed me some risqué pictures of the girls he dated. I thought, *What **the fuck**?* This guy wasn't lying about his escapades. Then I spotted one and froze. It was *Old Man's* current squeeze, *Lise*.

He explained that this one had his only child. However, *Lise* told *Old Man* that her baby's dad was dead. But this guy was alive and well and knew about his kid. I then drew a mental picture of her three-year-old daughter's face, then looked at *Kenny's* again. They were identical. *Old Man's* woman lied. *Kenny* was looking for his daughter.

I admitted that I knew her and that I had tried to date her sister. He then produced risqué pics of her as well. Then he showed me more pics of their aunt.

Kenny had screwed this girl's entire female family. He was a reckless

59

monster. No wonder she said he was dead. But he'd gotten to know me and played on my heartstrings. He cried and begged me to help him see his daughter.

I told him that I would see what I could do. Again, I was a man of my word. The moment I left, I immediately called *Old Man* and convinced him that the kid's dad was alive and that I met him in the joint. I admitted that this guy was a former *YBI* member and was now hustling for me to get back on his feet.

I also admitted that he was a scumbag who screwed every woman in her entire family. But I thought he deserved to see his daughter. *Old Man* had heard of him but didn't know anything about him. I somehow convinced him to let this guy see his kid, but on our terms.

Our terms were that *Kenny* could walk the kid up and down the block for twenty minutes and not take her out of our sight. If he

suddenly snapped and lost his mind and picked the kid up and ran, we agreed that we'd shoot him to protect the child.

We understood that we could have been putting the kid in harm's way, and that the kid could turn out to be collateral damage if *Kenny* tried anything. We hadn't thought it through. I just thought that any man who was that emotional about his kid deserved to spend some time with them even if it was only twenty minutes.

We had guns and were committed to shooting this guy if he tried anything or refused to return the kid. *Kenny* walked her up and down the block for about thirty minutes. We walked about fifteen paces behind him the entire time. When he was done, he turned the kid over and then wept like a baby. I was relieved that this went so smoothly.

Deep down, *Kenny* seemed to be an okay guy. He introduced me to a beautiful lesbian woman who lived across the street from him. She had very beautiful friends as well. She even made me a lot of drug money with her friends at the bank where she worked. She sold ounces every two days at work for me and never wanted a cut.

We hit it off well and started secretly dating. It was she who insisted that we keep our relationship a secret. So, I never said anything to anybody. *Kenny* and his friends had been trying to screw this girl for years. However, she convinced them that she wasn't interested in men and that she was a total lesbian. So, they laid off of her.

She even had a friend fly in from Ohio and introduced me. I was blown away by the friend's beauty. They took me to *Menjo's* (a well-known gay nightclub), where they drank and danced the night away (with each other). I sat at the table, feeling like the "king of queens," and sometimes watched in amazement as they openly flirted on the dance floor.

The girlfriend frequented Detroit and shared a story about a date she went on with *Hitman Hearns*. She said when marriage was brought up on that dinner date with his family, she simply asked someone to pass the salt (to change the subject). I laughed hysterically.

We went back to my house after drinking and dancing at the club. They drank, did some coke, and continued to enjoy the night. My sister burst into my room to be nosy and ruined the mood for me. So, we ended the party. The next day, the friend flew back to Ohio. She later

starred in a Spike Lee movie and went on to become a very well-known actress.

Kenny had gotten jealous and accused me of spending too much time with a lesbian who was never going to give it up. I got angry and tired of him calling her lesbian and other derogatory names, so I shared my secret with *Kenny*. That was a huge mistake because he went back and told her.

I guess she never wanted to hook up with any of those guys and used the gay excuse to avoid them. But then *Kenny* took it a step further and told all the guys in his neighborhood as well.

She was pissed at me for admitting that we were screwing. She told me she would never forgive me for exposing her personal business. She stopped calling, and I hadn't heard from her in three weeks. I was disappointed in myself. I stopped dealing with *Kenny* as well.

Then suddenly, she called and asked me to join her for dinner one night. I agreed but took my gun just in case. She knew too many neighborhood gangsters for me not to take precautionary measures. Luckily, I did. It turns out she lured me to a location where *Kenny* and a team of their friends were waiting to kill me. She had somehow convinced him that I should die for betraying her trust. *Kenny* was also pissed that I had stopped supplying him and contacting him.

I rode with her and had no idea where she was taking me. While she drove, I could since her anger building up. She began to express herself about the incident that had happened three weeks ago. I constantly explained that my intentions were to defend her honor from the awful names *Kenny* and his buddies were unleashing on her behind her back. But she wasn't trying to hear what I was saying. She was too hell-bent on revenge.

When we pulled up at a house near Linwood and Davison Avenue, there were about five of their mutual guy friends and a couple of women there. I was packing, and none of them knew it. It turns out I had provided *Kenny* with the gun that he was now going to use to kill me. I saw the butt hanging out of his pocket. He asked me to walk with him, so we left the house and walked down the street. It was about 10 p.m. and dark.

As we walked out of the house, I heard his buddies excitedly through the window saying, **"Kenny's about to do it."** They seemed suddenly nervous, but none of them attempted to stop it.

None of them knew I had a *Blue Steel*, long barrel .45 caliber in my waistband, and I never took my finger off of the trigger as we walked. I made sure to walk on his right side as the .45 was already aimed at him.

I could sense his hesitation as he tried hard to work up the nerve to carry out his plan. But I didn't shoot. He had his hand around my shoulder, crying, telling me how much he missed his little girl. It was as if he was having a flashback. I assured him that I had made it happen once and that I would try to make it happen again for him. All the while, I knew I would have to get off a shot before he did.

But I kept trying to calm him and defuse the situation. It was the only chance I had to keep him and/or me alive. I was mapping out a route just in case I had to shoot him. I wasn't that familiar with the Linwood/Davison area at the time. However, I knew that if anything happened, I couldn't go back to that house and would have to make my way to one of my closer spots.

Something came over him. He couldn't do it! He cried and constantly repeated that he wanted to see his daughter. I, again convinced him that I would try to make it happen. Perhaps it was my nurturing tone or his paternal sensitivities that changed his approach. Nevertheless, at that moment, this monster expressed compassion.

We walked back to the house from which we came. I did not go in I simply asked him to tell that dyke whore to come out and take me home. She didn't know that I was packing my *Blue Steel* .45 caliber. I imagined splattering her brains against that driver's side window but knew I probably wouldn't survive a fiery crash on the Lodge Freeway.

She lived, but I never saw her again, nor did I want any more of her business. I guess you could say she was as lucky as I was that night.

I never kept that promise to *Kenny* of arranging for him to see his little girl again. At that point, he could go through the courts as far as I was concerned. I was never going to dodge a bullet like that again from him.

Kenny died nearly four months after seeing his little girl. As dangerous as he was, and as much as I had come to despise him, I was

proud that I orchestrated one of his biggest wishes in his life before he died—to see his daughter. In a sense, I guess it was a dying wish of his that I had fulfilled.

CHAPTER XIV –
CONTEMPLATING AN EXIT

My father's image began to haunt me. I didn't want his dying last words spoken to me to be in vain. The words, "Take Care" began playing over and over in my head. I wanted to make good on them. I was, again, doing a lot of reflecting on my life and began subconsciously planning my exit from the game. I was constantly praying and having to lie to my companions and friends about my whereabouts.

My friends would call me, and I would say I was over at some chick's house just to get off the phone with them ... when in fact, I was often sitting in the back of a classroom at Marygrove College (where, ironically, I was admitted to the Griots program years later).

It didn't matter what the instructors were teaching—I was simply there to learn and assure myself that I could keep up with college students. I had to convince myself that I was just as smart as they were before I made my full transition. I would whisper my intentions to the instructors. I let them know of my desire to enroll in college one day soon. They never turned me away. Had they known I was a drug dealer, I'm sure they would have seen things a little differently. But they saw me as a nonstudent desperate to learn and make good of my life.

This would be the start of my efforts to make good on my father's last words ... to make certain that they weren't spoken in vain.

I was still hustling, but the burning desire to achieve any further success in the game was dying. My passion for learning and making good on my father's wish had grown exponentially within me. I wanted to learn anything I could in a classroom setting, and I was soaking up everything. The teachers seemed happy about my presence. They were albeit, unbeknownst to them, helping with my transformation from the drug dealer from the streets to the student in the classroom. And every chance I got, I hit the books like a normal student. I was a few years older than the other students, but I did not care. Things started lining up for me in mysterious ways.

The street team was always excited to see me when I resurfaced, but they knew something was off. I lacked the desire to pick up chicks

or go to the malls as before. I wasn't as eager to attend *Lions* or *Tigers*

games anymore.

It bothered me that I had never lived on campus—life-bonding with other students. And although my deep desire was to be a student now, I still had to keep my head in the game. I wasn't completely out of the streets, so I didn't have a choice. The team still relied on my supply, and I could still be killed at any given moment if I began slipping.

CHAPTER XV – THE NEAR MISS

I got a call from a guy who lived around the corner from me, named *Will*. I never liked this guy and knew he couldn't be trusted. Although my brother usually dealt with him, I always warned him about *Will*.

About a month earlier, I witnessed an incident that assured my suspicions about this guy. I had never known anyone living in this drug-infested neighborhood to drive around with 9mm Uzis in his trunk, get stopped by the cops, and drive away every time.

I saw *Will* being pulled over by the cops, so I parked at the gas station at the intersection of Greenfield and Plymouth Roads. I observed as the cops search his car one block over on Plymouth road near Winthrop. He was asked to exit the car. Officers looked in his back seat and under the front seat, then escorted him around to the rear of the car to pop the trunk. There was a short conversation between him and the cops prior to him opening the trunk.

When he opened his trunk, they conversed and laughed before they closed it and let him drive off. I discreetly followed Will as he headed home and pulled into his driveway. I called out the window to see if he was still interested in selling me the Uzi he'd tried to sell me a week or two earlier. He popped his trunk, presented the Uzi, and gave me a price of three hundred and fifty dollars. I thought to myself, You snitch fuck, then told him, **"I'll get back with you."**

So, when *Will* called me on my private line, I knew who I was dealing with, but I was shocked that he even had my phone number. He asked me if I would bring him an eighth of a kilo of cocaine. I asked how he got my phone number, and he couldn't recall. I insisted he tell me before we did any business. Then he said he thought my brother gave it to him. I asked him which one, and he said, *"I forgot. I think it was Old Man."* I told him I'd call him right back and hung up the line.

I immediately called *Old Man* and *Beast*, who were the only ones known to deal with *Will*. I asked if either of them had given *Will* my phone number. They assured me that they hadn't given *Will* my number. Once assured, there was no way I was going to deliver this guy anything. But my buddy, *Big Dex*, said, *"Yes , let's drop it off and make that money."* I warned *Big Dex* of the dangers of dealing with

Will. I half-jokingly said, *"There would probably be a house full of cops waiting on us to make that delivery."*

Big Dex was about six hundred pounds and promised to keep the sack in his underwear, under his balls, until the money was exchanged. He said there's no way they're going to check down there. I laughed and was hesitant, but agreed. But I insisted we do it my way. We would immediately hand it to *Will* to conduct the business with his own connect. We kept no drugs in the truck, and would negotiate nothing. That was going to be *Will's* job. I also advised *Big Dex* that under no circumstances were we to leave the truck.

When we got there (at an unknown house in the neighborhood), *Will* came out to the car and asked me to come in. I told him no and that he was to oversee all transactions, shoving the dope at him. He advised me that they wanted to talk to me. I told him that I wasn't interested and that he was *"The Man"* during this transaction, and that all negotiations went through him. As Will kept talking, I demanded he stop wasting our time and go get the deal done. I then rolled up the window. He went in to handle the transaction.

As he entered the house, I could see faces peering out the kitchen window as if they were anticipating me coming in.

Five minutes later, a woman came out and started raking the grass. I noticed she raked over areas with no leaves while coming closer and closer to the truck. But we had driven a buddy's truck with tinted windows, so I raised the windows so she couldn't see who was inside. We had no drugs, guns, or anything illegal in the truck, so I wasn't too concerned. At that point, I assumed these were cops.

Will finally came out, so I cracked the window slightly to hear him out. There was no way that I was going to let him place that dope back in the truck. He simply wanted to confirm the offer but hadn't made the exchange. He said they insisted on meeting me prior to any transactions—still expecting us to get out of the car and come in.

Big Dex got excited and told me he would go in, meet them, and get the money. As he gestured to get out of the truck, I grabbed him and said, **"Will's gonna handle this deal."** I then demanded that *Will* go back in and finish the deal. **"You are The Man,"** I assured him and rolled my window back up. I advised *Big Dex* that there was a

house full of cops waiting for us in there. He looked at me in disbelief. I told him to sit calmly while *Will* handled this deal.

Will looked at the tinted window in disbelief, then walked away. I could suddenly see the fear on *Big Dex's* face, as if we were now negotiating with cops, but *Will* was negotiating with them—not us! I didn't know the law that well but assured *Big Dex* that we had no drugs in the vehicle and that *Will* was just giving us the twenty-seven hundred dollars (the price of the eighth) that he owed us, if worse came to worst.

We waited for about eight minutes (which seemed like an eternity, considering). Then *Big Dex* broke the worried silence and asked, **"What if he doesn't come back out?"** I simply responded, **"We'll give him five more minutes, then we're out. We'll deal with him later for attempting to set us up."**

69

It only took two more minutes. *Will* came out and handed me a wad of cash. I'd sold a few eighths before, and a quick observation of the denominations and the size of the wad he handed me, assured me that this was way more than the $2700 asking price.

This was thousands. I peeled off a twenty-spot without a second thought. I handed that twenty dollars to *Will* (who was trying to delay me and asking me to make sure it was all there). Ignoring what he was saying, I drove off in a hurry and told *Big Dex*, excitedly, that this snitch handed me close to twenty thousand dollars in (what was surely) marked bills.

Nevertheless, we picked up my little sister and her friend. I asked if they wanted to go shopping in a nearby city. The girls didn't hesitate. They grabbed their purses, hopped in, and we jumped on I-94 and headed out of state to the nearest cities where the liquor was cheap.

There was no way this money was going to be traced back to me. We spent the majority of it on cases of liquor and Moët. The girls grabbed about five thousand dollars' worth of outfits. They weren't happy. They wanted more.

We had a big party when we got back with free booze. It was a big hit and did a lot for our public relations and street credit.

I think back on that moment and wonder how it would have turned out if we had gotten out of the car and gone into that house.

Would we have been charged with possession and attempting to distribute an entire kilo of cocaine (what they actually paid for) and sentenced as big-timers? Regardless, we got through it. We dodged another bullet.

I saw *Will* about a week later while stopped at a traffic light. He pulled beside me and said, in a clandestine low voice, smiling, **"You got over."**

I smiled back and said, ***"Yeah, you're really lucky we did!"***

Then pulled off, never to see him again.

Years later, I heard a story about a semi-truck rolling over onto a car on the Southfield Service Drive north of Plymouth Road. The car was crushed—all three passengers in the car were killed.

I later found out that it was *Will*, his younger sister, and his mom who were in that car and were killed. What a tragedy.

CHAPTER XVI –
JUDGEMENT DAY

Another life-changing event hit me like a ton of bricks in the form of a court order. I was summoned to appear in Circuit Court before *Judge Michael Talbot*. This was the same case that had cost me three days in the county jail earlier that year. This case simply would not go away.

I went before an extremely strict judge facing an intent-to-deliver charge. The charges were so serious that I was facing twenty years. My attorney told me that if the prosecutor offered me a plea deal, I should consider it.

I barely remembered the incident. I never should have rented that car from *Coffee*. Here I was, two years later, standing in a courtroom before a judge regarding the same incident that seemed to keep resurfacing. Because these packs of crack were individually wrapped during that stop, this turned into an ***intent-to-deliver*** charge. And because I was the driver, the case was pinned on me.

I had heard of *Judge Michael Talbot's* techniques and thought to myself, I'm fucked. He was one of two judges rumored to provide drug defendants an unfair option.

I was told that this judge would offer you an automatic sentence for the charge, or the bailiff would provide the defendant with one hundred pennies. The defendant had to throw them in the air and catch as many as he could. The number of pennies that hit the floor represented the number of years you would be sentenced.

To this day, I'll never understand my brother's reasoning when I asked him for money for an attorney. He advised me that if I went in there with a high-powered attorney, this judge would throw the book at me. With a court appointed attorney, he advised, it would look like I was a very petty dealer. This was asinine to me, but I couldn't afford *Garner* at the time, so I had no choice. He had the money and, as far as I was concerned, was playing Russian roulette with my life.

Most drug dealers in Detroit were tried in **Frank Murphy Hall of Justice,** not Circuit Court. Why was I in Circuit Court for this charge, and why was I facing this judge? I never knew the answers to those questions. But at that moment, I found myself before this judge

with a court appointed attorney. It was a losing situation all the way around.

In the back of my mind, I thought I would be lucky to get out of there with a five-year sentence. But, like every other drug defendant, I genuinely believed that I was smart and could do better in society than being locked away in a cage.

My naivety kicked in, and suddenly jail was not the best option for me. I had to convince the judge of this and make him understand why it was not the best option for me. I was hopeful that I would walk out of there a free man—with fines and penalties, of course, but a free man.

As the proceedings began, I listened to my attorney plead my case.

I felt so helpless and frightened.

As he proceeded, the judge asked him to approach the bench. I had no idea what was going on. This lawyer came back excitedly and exclaimed that I could strike a deal in exchange for six years and advised that, with good behavior, I could be out in three and a half years.

Just then, for some strange reason, I felt enlightened. I guessed they had stopped the whole penny thing as unconstitutional or a civil rights violation. Whatever the reason, I didn't have to go through that. I was now being sentenced like a human being. But I had never been to prison before, only local lockup, and this guy sounded like an idiot to me for coming back and proposing a jail sentence.

If they were willing to negotiate on my future, I wanted a say in it. I told the attorney that I had never served time and that the offer was too harsh. I could not accept it. He headed back to the bench to give the judge the news.

I must have looked a little more confident in that courtroom because I felt a sudden sense of power. I was negotiating my future with this suburban white male judge who had exerted his power and will over so many wasted black lives before me. I would make him feel different today. I just knew it.

I would be just as important in his life today as anyone else he knew. I would make him see me for who I could be, and not for who I was in the past.

Suddenly, my attorney approached me again, smiling with another offer. He excitedly said, ***"Thirty-six months. You'll be out in eighteen months with good behavior."***

Again, I rejected it! I told this two-bit attorney to stand there and repeat in five-second intervals: ***"Thirty-six months is too harsh."*** He looked at me like I was crazy. I said, "Start now!" He began, while I asked the judge, ***"May I speak, Your Honor?"***

While I spoke, everyone in the courtroom could hear the attorney in a low-toned voice murmuring, ***"Thirty-six months is too harsh,"*** repeatedly like a parrot. I was in total charge of my defense.

I implored the judge to take into consideration who I was, where I was, and what surrounded me. I told him about my best friends who were murdered in a house we frequented (I didn't admit it was my dope spot.) He probably already knew and had the obituaries in his hand to prove it.

Nonetheless, these streets were my reality. I had to project it in a manner that he understood and empathized with. I painted this picture vividly and portrayed my world to him in living color.

I was almost certain that the only experience he had in my world was through the nightly news, his subscription to *The New York Times*, or from behind his bench.

I must have gone on for twenty minutes before he intervened. This time, he presented an offer in the form of an ultimatum. I was eager to hear him out. He looked me directly in my eyes and said, ***"If you can pass a drug test today, I will let you walk out of my courtroom and drop all the charges against you."***

My heart dropped to my stomach. I was ecstatic. I even smiled and eagerly said, ***"Yes, Your Honor. I'll take it at anytime."***

I was confident because I had been dropping urine six months prior to appearing in his courtroom. For the first two months, I had a toothache, and I put cocaine on the tooth to numb the pain. It must have come back in my urine and been documented in my records for the judge to know this. But I knew I didn't use it, and that it was not in my system now. So, I agreed and knew I would pass the test with flying colors.

I assured him that I could pass the test. I was confident that the cocaine was in my system. I let him know I would be ready to drop urine anytime he scheduled it. He advised me to come past his bench and into his chambers to drop at that very moment. I said, ***"Sure, Your Honor"***

As I walked past his bench heading to his chambers, I was feeling ecstatic because I knew I didn't use cocaine. But suddenly, I was nervous again. I remembered that I had smoked marijuana a few days prior to my court appearance. I suddenly stopped on the side of the bench and asked in a whispered tone, **"Does weed count, Your Honor?"** He assured me that it did.

I then admitted that I couldn't do it and stood frozen. He stared at me, face-to-face, for about thirty seconds, then broke his silence.

He advised me that I was a smart young man and ordered me to enroll in school somewhere—anywhere. He then adamantly told me to get out of his courtroom but warned me that if I committed any crimes from that moment forward, he would personally request me in his courtroom to face sentencing. And that he would be responsible for the extent of my punishment.

He also promised me that any crime I committed (even stealing a stick of bubble gum), he would make sure that I would serve out the entire twenty-year sentence for this initial crime.

I shed a tear or two as I absorbed the moment. This white, upper-class, mean, educated man had just spared my life. I asked him if I could hug him before I left the courtroom a free man, and he obliged.

It was a meaningful, tight embrace. I felt I loved him like a father figure, and I would not let him down.

CHAPTER XVII – THE MOTIVATION

Life went on. I was visiting classes more frequently to continue boosting my confidence. My intent was clear; returning to school was my full objective. I really had no choice. I was in my late twenties but could see a little further ahead in life now. It was clear that there was a positive future on my horizon.

I had pretty much handed the game over to the guys. However, any deals going down that were worth more than three thousand dollars I orchestrated. I needed some cash. Besides, I usually provided the goods and was rarely present during these transactions anyway.

There was simply too much money left on the table. But I had to be extremely careful. My freedom for the next twenty years of my life depended upon it.

Everything I did now triggered thoughts about the judge's warning. I was extremely careful about who I dealt with. All my friends were now suspicious and were getting a second once-over. I had to be sure there were no snitches in my very tight circle.

I did well. My goal now was to make sure that I had money to look decent going to school and had decent transportation to get there and back.

Then came the turning point that changed everything for me and catapulted me to the fast track of enrollment.

I got a call from *Big Dex* for a request to deliver an eighth of a kilogram. We were already in the neighborhood. But first, I needed to stop at the barbecue joint at the corner of Plymouth Road and St.

Mary's Street to get their famous *rib tips*, which I always ordered. But for some strange reason, tonight I got the half slab. I had never gotten a half-slab before.

It was about 10 p.m. when *Big Dex* and I grabbed the food, then drove to deliver the goods. Two blocks away from our destination, we were pulled over on Mansfield Street, north of Plymouth Road, by narcotics officers. This was the K-9 unit. *Big Dex* panicked and put the

eighth of a kilo in his pants. I told him to give it to me, slid it into the box under the half slab, shut the box, and placed it on the back seat.

The officers made us exit the car. They had the dogs sniff us thoroughly... nothing! Then they guided the dog to the car while we sat on the curb. The dog sniffed around the tires and under the car... nothing! They then opened the car doors and led the dog to sniff inside. All four doors were opened. As we sat on the curb, we had a clear view of where the dog sniffed. My heart was beating out of my chest when the dog sniffed the food. He barked when he sniffed the barbecue. We watched the officer open the box, then shut it back. They put the dog away, uncuffed us, and told us to enjoy our night before leaving.

We looked at each other. I promised *Big Dex* at that moment that I was done with the game and would be going back to school full-time. He laughed. I don't know if he believed me, but it happened a few months later. Getting away that last time assured me of just how costly a simple mistake could be. I could no longer sacrifice myself nor could I let *Judge Michael Talbot* down. I was done with the game for good!

CHAPTER XVIII – THE SWITCH

I learned about the Coleman A. Young School on Monroe Street in downtown Detroit (Greektown). It offered first-time offenders a chance to get their GEDs. I enrolled and attended faithfully.

The tutors were so impressed by my efforts and abilities that I was assigned a mentor position to teach some of the other students. Here I was, without a diploma, tutoring first-time offenders. I started off having them read simple sentences from a book that was provided to me. I was offended by the third-grade material they had given me.

Nevertheless, I had the students taking turns reading the passages aloud. I noticed that some were struggling with three and four-letter words. I laughed softly, thinking the joke was on me, but it was real. It was an "aha" moment for me. I could not believe their reading levels. I went home and privately cried. After all the struggles and advancements over the years, some of us were still this far behind.

Martha Rodger was a tutor at the school. I noticed her right away. She was a graduate from the University of Michigan and graduated at the top of her class. She had previously retired from teaching in a suburban district in northern Michigan. She now dedicated most of her free time tutoring us first-time offenders. She worked full-time for *Mr. Gabriel Werba*, who owned a public relations firm at the Renaissance Center. The company was located in the Renaissance Building so Martha would make the trek two to three days weekly to the school to tutor. *Martha* took a special interest in me.

She had a bounce in her step that amazed me for an older woman. Her walk gave me the impression that she was extremely happy and didn't have a care in the world. My first impression of *Martha* was that she was a committed woman who really enjoyed life.

She often came to the center during her lunch hour and spent two hours tutoring us. *Martha* was so committed to teaching that she sometimes bought students calculators, bookbags, and occasionally food. I found it odd that this suburban woman from Royal Oak went above and beyond her duties to help us. Between her time assisting *Mr. Werba* at his firm, *Durocher, Dixon & Werba*, she faithfully made her way to the Coleman A. Young School to volunteer weekly.

She was eager to tutor me because of my willingness to learn. I was so determined at this point that I wanted to make anyone who met me proud of my drive and achievements. Therefore, Martha took exceptional interest and a lot of pride in helping me. She could not have known what motivated me, and I didn't care. I had *Judge Michael Talbot's* words as well as my dad's engraved in my mind. I had to succeed. It wasn't out of fear at this point but commitment and self-pride. I was prepping for college—I was determined to be a college student.

I aced the G.E.D. exam. I scored extremely high on that test. *Martha* immediately helped me enroll at Wayne County Community College (WC3) on Fort Street in downtown Detroit. We had to keep the momentum going.

She was a godsend. Each year during the summer, we would travel across the U.S. with a Madison Heights senior group, consisting mostly of elderly and middle-aged white folks. Besides the driver, I was always the only Black guy on these excursions. But it didn't matter. This was a new world to me, and I loved it. I've always had an old soul, and these people were my peers at that time, and they were hilarious. They made me laugh so hard at times that I thought I'd wet my pants.

Once I visited Mount Vernon with this group. After we were given the tour we returned to the main house. One of the women was so tired that she moved the ropes and sat at the table. Everyone looked at her and laughed, then she pulled out a seat for me to sit. Before you knew it, all the chairs were occupied. As we drank wine, jokes and laughter filled the air for about an hour. The curator stood there, unconcerned about our actions. It was amazing.

When we got up from the table, we went out back to survey the land. There were three or four rocking chairs lined up on the back porch overlooking the marsh area. This was the most spectacular landscape that I'd ever seen in my life. I asked the curator if I could sit for a moment. She moved the rope, and I sat. When I came to, the entire group was staring at me laughing. I'd gotten so comfortable that I'd fallen asleep. The curator said the particular chair that I sat in was believed to be George Washington's favorite chair. With that view, it was no wonder why it was his favorite. I hated it when these excursions were over. That was a fun bunch of guys.

Again, *Martha* was so impressed with me during her tutelage that she told her boss about me. I was then invited to the Renaissance to meet *Mr. Gabriel Werba* himself. My first impression of him was amazing. I remembered him talking so meticulously when he spoke, and he never wasted a word. I had a habit of losing myself blabbering at times. So, I had to pay particular attention to the way I spoke when I was around him so that I didn't embarrass myself.

I enrolled in Wayne County Community College (WC3) in the summer of 1991. During lunch breaks, *Mr. Werba* and *Martha* insisted that I come to his office to study. They said I would have privacy there.

I was ecstatic and usually ran to the People Mover at Cass and Fort Street and headed to the Renaissance Center during my breaks. Sometimes I simply walked. It didn't matter when or how long my breaks were between classes; they insisted I come to their office whenever I got the chance. I took full advantage of this opportunity.

Martha was always available, and we would study in the main conference room every time I got there.

The conference room was surrounded by glass walls and was situated near the center of the office. Although the office was never crowded, save for *Mr. Werba's* associates during his meetings, there was always a clear view of anyone in there. Whatever secretarial duties Martha had, they were always put on hold or done during short intermissions of our studies.

What amazed me most of all was that when I came, sometimes there were five or six white businessmen in suits sitting in the conference room in deep discussion. But they always wrapped up their meetings when they saw me enter the office. Not once did I have to wait more than five minutes upon arrival. They sometimes rushed to clear the room. I was embarrassed and told *Martha* I could wait or study elsewhere. She insisted that *Gabe (Mr. Werba)* wanted me to have that room when I came and downplayed my concerns.

I became a part of that team for as long as it took me to get my associate's degree. I loved that office and the people. Occasionally, the design firm in their office would provide me with temporary work at their separate Troy office to earn extra cash. I would make about three

hundred dollars for three hours of work folding small boxes. They looked like jewelry boxes.

When *General Motors* moved into the building, *Durocher, Dixon & Werba* relocated from the 27th floor to the 23rd floor. It was only a four-story difference. I would occasionally go to the office during twilight hours or during the fireworks. During that time, the steady lights in the distance (across the river in Canada) appeared to be blinking. I was so amazed at its beauty that I wrote a poem about the elevator ride up, titled ***FIGHT***.

As I am elevated 27 floors in the Ren Cen, I hear the twinkling lights in the distance,

An audience applauding my premature achievements ... I ascend to my destination.

The deafening applause sees the war as won, and the victory lap nearer. But the race has only begun, and my real battle awaits.

The toll bell "Rings," and the lights grow silently dim,

The pathway opens ... And leads me to where I continuously prepare for war.

—Larry Snell

Durocher Dixson & Werba eventually left the Renaissance Building and relocated directly across Jefferson Avenue, facing the General Motors Building. The inspiring view from my ride up the elevator was gone. However, lots of things inspired me to write or sink into passionate thoughts. And poetry comforted me and allowed me to express my sensitive side ... I find this very necessary in this life.

A couple of my favorite poems ever written are Edna St. Vincent Millay's *There's No Frigate Like a Book* and Dorothy Parker's *The Little Old Lady in Lavender Silk.*

Edna St. Vincent Millay's poem takes me to places I had never been, while Dorothy Parker's poem seemed to juxtapose my perspective into the woman's mind. Besides, they are both very fun to read.

My buddy, Trino Sanchez, the *Why Am I So Brown* author, introduced me to the poetry circuit. I frequently read poetry in front of audiences at Union Street, Stuart's, and other venues around Detroit. I once attended an Oakland University event for the release of the book of poetry, *Passages North.* I was hooked. There's nothing like an author reciting their material. It's so passionate and personal.

God bless *Trino Sanchez.* We became inseparable during my early college years. He was older but loved my potential, and I loved his work. He also valued our friendship as much as I did.

He dragged me around the city, introducing me to multicultural events weekly. After five years of friendship, as I stood in his kitchen, I noticed a risqué magazine on the table. As I looked at it in shock, he suddenly appeared and began to sob. He admitted his secret to me after all these years. I hugged him to comfort him. I assured him that I loved him just the same. We continued our embrace and laughed. He laughed through his tears.

CHAPTER XIX –
A REAL MENTOR

Nothing about my visits changed. I'd grown extremely close to both *Martha* and *Gabe*. I passed each semester with a 3.5 GPA and above. Following every semester, things were becoming clearer. It was as if I was in The Matrix. I was passing classes with ease. Humanities became my favorite subject.

I was suddenly interested in the arts. Historic and thought-provoking artworks were now the most beautiful things in the world to me. It was as if my soul was jolted every time I saw a good painting. I was taken back to that time period and place. This was weird but it became my new normal.

Gabriel Werba was a very interesting character. He spoke seven different languages, fluently. He handed me a brochure detailing his life. It read like an oil painting. His mom fled Germany with him and his sister during the Holocaust. They made their way to France before coming to the United States. I guess that kind of pressure would force you to "ace" where you aimed, which probably explained why he was so successful. I read the brochure, and I was flabbergasted by his journey. I bonded with him and Martha from the moment I met them.

Gabe always had a smile when he talked to me and always made perfect sense in everything he said. I was in awe of him at this point and hung on to every word he shared. I listened intently to everything and tried to memorize all the advice he gave me.

He invited me to a Detroit Tigers baseball game once, and there were about six or seven other men who sat around us when we arrived. They all greeted him with amazement, as if he had just walked across the river to get there. My assumption was that, if they knew this guy, they were probably very important people—successful stockbrokers or something. They certainly looked the part.

Gabe once gave me an opportunity to join a stock competition. I was to pick ten stocks and, depending on how they performed over a three-month period, I could win ten thousand dollars. I came in third place out of 100. I was excited but did not know how I came that close. Since then, my stock selection sucked.

These men gathered around *Gabe* (*Mr. Werba*), and they paid very little attention to the game. They were questioning him about investments and politics. They got extremely quiet and leaned in when he responded. The level of attention he commanded still amazes me.

But then, I thought about the brochure and thought to myself: This guy was the president of America Mensa. It's no wonder he never wasted a word—he had none to waste.

We left the game in the bottom of the eighth inning with the *Tigers* leading by one, and the guys followed us out. I do not remember if the *Tigers* held on to win that game or not. But this group of guys appeared to be entertained only by the presence of *Gabe* (*Mr Werba*). They interacted with him about social issues and investments and hung on to his every word like classroom students the entire time.

Like I said, he was a very interesting man.

He and *Martha* had somehow arranged for me to attend a writer's course at Middlebury College in Vermont. I researched the demographics and, at the time, found that the Black population represented less than one percent. There was no way I was going to Vermont.

I based my decision solely on fear. Had I understood the bigger picture then, I would not have hesitated and would have attended. I always wanted to be a writer. If I had gone, I'd probably have ten best

86

sellers under my belt by now. Maybe I would have learned different writing styles or something. Nonetheless, like a fool, I decided not to go.

When I recognized some of the writers and authors who had attended that college, my heart sank even deeper. I often wonder how that journey would have impacted my life. But I let the effects of my past interfere with my decision-making process in the present.

Gabe (Mr. Werba) would occasionally have me drop off reports to a guy named *Larry Doss* in the Sherwood Forest district in Detroit. *Larry Doss* would invite me in and offer me a soda or something when I stopped by. I rarely accepted. Once, I took him up on the offer. I was trying not to be rude by refusing so often. I was in awe as I stepped inside and saw the renowned attorney, *Johnny Cochran* of the O.J. Simpson's Dream Team sitting at the table.

I had never really considered anyone as a role model. But *Gabe* was so interesting and had interesting friends. My admiration for him had nothing to do with his circle of friends, but his character and compassion. And, to me, judging by how he interacted with everyone else, it was evident that he had an amazing impact on their lives as well. I strangely wanted to be as close to him as I could. He had become my first real role model.

When his mom died, I felt horrible. *Gabe* was such a good guy, and I hated to see him suffer during her loss. He invited me to her funeral service and appeared to be managing his loss quite well.

She must have been in her nineties and had apparently lived a long and prosperous life. I recalled from his brochure how she fled from Germany with him and his sister, then eventually made it to the United States prior to her stay in France. I had never met her in life, but strangely, I felt as if I knew her personally in death during the services.

87

During the burial, he took the shovel and scooped up two shovelfuls of earth and dumped them on the lowered casket, then gestured the shovel toward me. I looked at *Ann Marie* and *Dean (Mr. Werba's* kids) to gauge their reactions, but they didn't seem to mind. So, I got up and mimicked Gabe. I took two scoops of earth and dropped them on the lowered casket as well.

Here I was, being handed the shovel to put dirt on his mother (a true survivor of the Holocaust) during her passage ... and by the president of *American Mensa*, who was now my friend and mentor. I was totally honored and at a loss for words.

To this day, when I lose the people closest to me, I stay behind to cover them as much as I can before the dump trucks approach. It soothed me during Mom's and *Justin's* (my nephew) losses.

I saw *Dean (Gabe's son)* years later, after *Gabe's* death. We decided to meet up at a bar. He brought a friend. We drank merrily. I just wanted to talk about his father and express to him the impact his dad had on my life and others. He never followed his dad's professional path in life but expressed to me that he wished he had.

We spoke of *Gabe* as if he were a character in a folklore tale. I missed him and was so proud to call him my friend. *Dean* admitted that he may have been naïve about the impact his dad had on so many

others. But he missed him and wished he could have a mulligan. However, there are no do-overs in life. Death is absolutely final.

I looked at his headstone and thought to myself that it should have stood out above any other headstone in that cemetery. He was the president of American Mensa (for God's sake), he had friends in high places, and he was special to me.

But then I remembered, he drove an older Honda Accord and never used or wanted a computer. He conducted all his business with a notebook, a pencil, and a secretary.

In the end, I think he would be satisfied blending in—he needed no extravagant ornaments to monument his life or his death. I'm sure his contributions were enough for him. And I was certain that, had he wanted a twenty-foot bronze statue in his likeness, his friends and family would have carried out those wishes. I guessed a small headstone was all he wanted.

Years later, just when I thought I could not admire him anymore, I pulled up his tiny headstone on the internet, and it triggered more emotions of admiration. I wept again.

CHAPTER XX –
THE ADVANCED LEVEL

*G*abe's wife, *Berrie*, was on Orchestra Hall's board of directors and occasionally provided tickets for *Martha* and *me* to attend classical entertainment events. My cultural knowledge was widening. I began a love affair with classical music, musicals, and plays.

Martha and I once attended a play at the Attic Theatre with tickets as a gift from *Berrie*. The play stood out as my favorite—not because it was a metered rhyme play that went on for nearly two hours, but because it was a premiere. Wine and cheese were served during intermission, and the actors ran about and mingled with the audience. I had never been involved with anything like this. It was a fantasy come true.

Martha's daughter, *Stacey*, joined us that night. The play was called

The Misanthrope *by Molière.*

At intermission, *Stacey* and I went outside to breathe some night air and abandon the bustle for a bit. It was a beautiful night. As we chatted and enjoyed our break, we both noticed a man standing about ten feet away in a shadow of darkness, leaning against the building, apparently on the same mission—to get away from the festivities for a while.

We were a little startled, and I apologized to him for (I guessed) breaking the monotony of his night. It was apparent that he wanted to get away from everyone and was clearly enjoying the quiet night air. In a low tone, he said, **"No need to apologize,"** and continued in an *English* accent, **"The night air is wonderful tonight."**

Stacey nudged me, urging me to look down in the direction of his shoes. As I looked, *Stacey* began to laugh. I had to think fast and interrupted her laughter by talking about how much I was also enjoying the night air. Then I mentioned to him that his shoes were quite different and interesting from any pair I'd ever seen before. He looked down at them, as if he had just noticed them himself, and said, **"Yes, they are family heirlooms. They were handed down to me."**

Stacey embarrassingly giggled a little more. Thankfully, it was time to go back in and enjoy the second half of the show. I wished the man

a wonderful rest of his night. We then walked back into the theatre and took our seats.

Before intermission ended, there was a ceremonial announcement by a Hudson's representative. Hudson's Department Store was the proud sponsor of the play. The representative gave a speech and then introduced *Lord Wedgwood* from England. He was visiting Detroit to honor Hudson's and presented them with a half-million-dollar pottery piece from his family's stock. The Wedgewoods establishment was a well known pottery company in England.

I was amazed as I looked at the man who, just five minutes ago, was standing outside explaining to me where his shoes came from. I looked over at *Stacey*, and her jaw literally dropped as she stood looking goofily at *Lord Wedgwood* making the announcement and presenting the pottery donation.

The events of the play that night are memories engraved in my mind forever—not just because of what happened that night, but also because of what happened the following Thursday during my final exam.

I was really worried about passing the exam, but I was confident that, when the time came, I would pass. My test phobia kicked in, but I was determined. I shot for an A, but was expecting nothing less than a B minus.

My teacher announced that the extra bonus question represented twenty-five percent of the final exam. If I can ace this bonus question at twenty-five percent of my grade, I thought, I will score nothing less than an A-minus … I just knew it.

As we prepared to take the final exam, the teacher read the bonus question aloud as she handed out the test. The bonus question was: **"What family from England is famously known for their pottery since the early 1300s?"**

I nearly fainted. I had spoken with *Lord Wedgwood* just three days ago. I was going to ace this test, and I knew it when she finished the question. Then, I looked at the test, and my confidence soared. I scored an A -plus. My new life was coming into focus. My world was broadening.

I finished junior college and graduated with a 3.5 *GPA* and with an Associate of Liberal Arts degree. I was doing well. If Judge *Michael Talbot* could see me now, I thought he would really be proud.

He had spared me from his bench, and I was now making the most of it. As the first in my family, I now had a college degree and was headed to a university to achieve a four-year degree.

Martha helped me do some research, and we found that Wayne State University was offering a scholarship for their *Journalism Institute for Minority (JIM)* program. I had to have that scholarship. I knew I could not pay for college. I wanted an English degree, not a Journalism degree, but this was a free ride and just what I needed

CHAPTER XXI –
NO LIMITS TO TRUE LOVE

My father and mother were not scholars and didn't put away money for our college. With ten kids, they didn't have the means. Nevertheless, as I look back, I know just how special they were. They provided us with everything they could. Dad occasionally took the boys hunting and fishing, while Mom nurtured and cared for us all, unconditionally. They truly dedicated their lives to us. They never separated through all the kids and all the years prior to their deaths.

My mom was a nurse's assistant when I was young. Her maternal instincts were always evident. Therefore, no matter what our issues were, she solved them. She always had a more lenient, nurturing response to any problems we had. We preferred to deal with her rather than Dad, who was the authoritarian of the household. We always preferred the easy way out of everything.

My dad was the breadwinner. He was a military man and encouraged us all to enter the military. Since there were no college funds put away, he advised us that the military would provide the foundation for anything we needed in life.

My brother *Hickey* bought it hook, line, and sinker. He could not wait to graduate high school to join the military. I always preferred going to college. I thought if there was a will, there would be a way. I was not interested in joining the military. As a young boy, I always saw college as the only alternative to a struggling life.

My dad spent more than ten years in the military and saw some combat in Korea. He had a knife wound from his shoulder that went across his spine to the opposite side of his tailbone. He and all four of his brothers were military guys. *Uncle James* retired and was so good with his finances that he'd accumulated at least a couple million dollars in money and assets. When we visited his family, it was special—not because he was rich, but because he was hilarious.

Uncle James always made us laugh. He appeared so regal to me. I didn't know until his funeral that he was a ladies' man. He was married to a beautiful, tall German woman—my *Aunt Brenda*. But all the women he was dating had attended his funeral. It was quite

embarrassing for my aunt because it appeared everyone else in Indiana knew about these women. But *Aunt Brenda* either hid the embarrassment well or simply didn't care. Because, in the end, she had the last laugh. She ended up with most of his assets.

My dad was a cement mason. So, his work was seasonal. However, he did find work during the colder months as well. I remember him spending time at the union hall when work wasn't as readily available.

He was loved and very popular at that union hall. He had ten kids and a beautiful wife. There was this guy named *Rawhide* who was there. He stands out to me because he would always make a pass at my mom when she went there to pick up my dad.

She would occasionally pick my dad up from the union hall because he sometimes gambled away all his money. I hated Rawhide for liking my mom. It was obvious he was jealous of my dad, and everyone knew it. Even in her older age and with many kids, my mom was still a looker.

Going to the union hall to pick up my dad on payday had almost become a weekly routine. The men started drinking after work, then the gambling would begin. Dad was always late coming home on Fridays. After a while, my mom assumed they had to be cheating my dad out of his money because he'd lose quite often. So, she began sitting there and letting him gamble for an hour or two. She sat with him to make sure the games were fair.

Suddenly, with her supervision, he began winning more often. *Rawhide* got pissed once and told my dad to shut up and cursed him for having my mom babysit him while he gambled. My dad was drunk and laughed. Just then, Rawhide hauled off and punched my dad in the mouth. My mom was in shock and called him a bully and cursed him. There were guys at the table warning *Rawhide* that he may have hit the wrong guy. *Rawhide* shrugged it off as if he was ready for anybody. It was known that he always carried a .38 on his hip.

My mom gathered my dad's winnings as she continued to curse *Rawhide*, then helped my dad to the car. His mouth was bleeding, but he was okay. I guess the whiskey took away a lot of the shock and pain of being cold-cocked. They headed home. Little did that crowd of about fifty people know that my brothers and brother-in-law were planning revenge.

At the union hall, about an hour and twenty-five minutes passed uneventfully. *Rawhide* sat there, convinced that he was king of, not only the union hall, but the streets as well. He knew my father had sons and thought they knew better than to come to the union hall and start trouble. Besides, there were so many of his friends and others in the hall at the time that he wasn't concerned about retaliation.

He should have listened to his friends and left.

My brothers and brother-in-law had all the doors on the outside manned while the men were still gambling inside. Three of them went inside. Two stood with shotguns guarding the front entrance, while one opened the back door to let in the others.

They showed their guns so that no one would attempt to run out. They were all inside while one stood outside. They brandished an Uzi, AK, and shotguns. When everything was secured, one of them yelled, **"We are not here to rob you, but we want to know where Rawhide is!"** About five people at one table pointed him out. They asked *Rawhide* to stand up.

They dragged him into the middle of the hall and beat him to a pulp. They took his money and his gun. They then told him that if he ever laid a hand on my dad or his friends again, they would kill him next time. They asked if he understood while he sat bleeding and swollen. He said, *"Clearly."*

My mom and dad continued to gamble at the union hall. There was never another bullying incident. The workers had a ball chatting and gambling for years afterward. They even welcomed *Rawhide* back. He hugged and kissed my father, and they continued a more genuine friendship.

My father never gave us much money, but he was adventurous and loved to take us ice fishing, smelt fishing, and hunting. I hated all of it. I felt sorry for the fish and always skipped rocks across the water to prevent them from being caught. My brothers would beg my father to leave me home because they loved fishing. But he wouldn't. He said I needed to bond with nature like everyone else. Although ice fishing was an interesting hobby, I loathed it most of all. Why would anyone drive a car on the ice to catch fish? In my eyes, he sacrificed his entire family for the dangerous and mundane exploration of ice fishing. It made no sense to me—even as a child.

However, he was a good dad who did things with us all the time. People loved him. Even his friends made things happen for us. They would do anything for Dad. He had a friend who owned a huge mobile home. Every year, he and my dad planned multi-state excursions. Sometimes, we were in the most beautiful areas in Canada, camping for days. Other times, we would be in New York or Montana on nature routes. It was great.

He had another friend, *Joe Brock*, who owned a Cessna airplane. It seemed like once a week, he would ask my dad if he wanted to fly. My dad loved flying and always joined him. My brothers and sisters would join them occasionally, but my mom and I never went up. I just wanted to play with my friends. My mom was terrified of flying.

I would ask them to fly over the railroad tracks where my buddies and I rode our bikes. They would do flyovers, and we were amazed to see them. We raced on our bikes to keep them in sight. Every now and then, they flew so low that we could see them waving through the windows.

My dad had very little but could do anything. People often asked him to repair their walkways or do some carpentry work for them, which he usually did and rarely charged them. Even now, my uncle calls my dad a genius and says there was nothing he couldn't do.

For some strange reason, my dad was tougher on me than on all my brothers. It was probably because I was the youngest. But I loved him anyway. I loved him so much that I would wait until he was asleep, then hug and kiss him. He'd start drinking and fall asleep, so I wasn't worried about him waking up. He couldn't be tough on me while he slept. I could show him as much love and affection as I wanted, and he couldn't do anything about it.

Again, when he died of cancer, I was only seventeen years old. I remember feeling so isolated when he was in the ICU. Everyone was there, but I felt alone. I had not lost anyone that close to me, and he was dying. We sat in the hallway at the hospital as he came in and out of consciousness.

When he would lose consciousness, my siblings and others would break out in light screams and cries, but when he came to, they celebrated with laughter and hugs. I, on the other hand, cried like crazy when he came to. But was silent while he lost consciousness. It was

because, while he was under, I was too busy begging God to bring him back. And when he came to, I was elated with tears and gratitude.

I thought it was strange that, of all my siblings present at the hospital, my mom was giving him a play-by-play account of my emotions and reactions. He suddenly asked for me before he lost consciousness for the last time. I was there alone with him. My mom made sure no one interfered. He looked at me with glossy eyes and managed to put a strained smile on his face. Then he spoke his last words to me. They were: *"TAKE CARE!"*

I would later find out that, even in death, he had given me the greatest gift that any father could have given his son.

CHAPTER XXII –
THE IMPACT OF HIS DYING WORDS

When I applied for the scholarship at Wayne State University's *(JIM)* Journalism Institute for Minorities, or The Journalism Institute for Media Diversity Program, depending on when you joined, I was hopeful. Writing was my strong suit. Of the twenty finalists, only two spots were available. Therefore, only two people would be selected for admission into the program. The panel of professors asked us to write a five-page essay on any subject that impacted our drive to become journalists.

I thought about what they wanted and what could I present.

Judging from their request, there had to be an angle.

I was thinking too hard. I settled down and thought about what I was most passionate about. Just then, it hit me, and I began scribbling. We had an hour to complete the task. I finished in forty-five minutes.

When everyone was done writing, we left the classroom and waited in the hallway as the panel entered and seated themselves. We could see through the door window as they passed the stories around from one faculty member to the next. When they finished reading them, we were asked to re-enter the classroom and be seated. I was anxious. I examined their faces for any indication of pleasure, excitement, disdain ... just something!

Then suddenly, they started tearing up, reaching for Kleenex. One of them spoke. She said, *"All the stories were great,"* and continued, *"but two of them were exceptionally impactful. And those are the two we chose."* I hoped one of them was mine.

The announcement came a day later. I WAS IN.

There were so many deterrents that challenged me when I accepted that scholarship. The night before my first day of class, I had a nightmare that was so real. The dresser and nightstand were falling near my head. I jerked and switched to avoid them. I could feel my body jerking in my sleep. I was in a shallow area between consciousness and sleep the entire night but could not open my eyes to see the flying objects. When I finally awakened, I remember being exhausted. Regardless, I made it to school on time.

One of the stipulations of the scholarship was that I maintain a

3.0 GPA. I thought this would be a cinch. I graduated from WC3 with a 3.5 GPA. I had nothing to worry about. I chose a "Bible as Literature" class as one of the electives. I thought this would be an easy three credit hours course. I knew I hated that class from the first day I entered. I never should have taken it or should have saved it for my senior year.

The teacher was weird. Every two minutes, she sipped her water bottle the entire class period. At the end of the class, the bottle was still full.

This class was nothing like a church sermon. Hell, the objective appeared to simply challenge everything you believed about God or religion. The teacher was an atheist and imposed her will and ideas from the onset. Her beliefs didn't bother me, but she never allowed anyone the opportunity to debate or dispute anything she said.

I had the opportunity to drop that class without penalty. And I attempted to do just that. During the second week, I'd had enough and walked out. I was going to the dean's office to advise him of my perception of the class and my decision to drop it. But my buddy came running down the hall after me. He begged me not to let this old woman deter me from getting those three easy credit hours. Like a fool, I listened to him, turned around, and went back. I was on probation after my first semester because of the "D" grade she had given me.

I met her in her office and tried to look menacing, hoping my appearance would force her to change my grade. She stood firm as I argued my point. I had scored no less than a B-minus on any of her assignments, but she replied that my attendance weighed heavily on my final "D" grade. I was stuck with that "D" and had to work my butt off to get off probation.

The JIM program was great. The old heads from the two major newspapers—The Detroit News and The Detroit Free Press, were teaching a lot of the courses.

Most of them were on strike from the newspapers, so the companies hired scab workers to fill the voids. This had gone on for so long that the old heads weren't blocking the entrances of The Detroit News and Free Press buildings anymore. They had given up. It was apparent the companies had no intention of bringing the staff workers back.

We benefited greatly from the program because so many former newspaper journalists continued teaching our courses. Some were even hired as part of the school's faculty. Those great writers were also lecturing during our annual retreats held at the old Red Cross estate. Those two-day retreats were wonderful. Most of us attended and got to know each other very well. It was an hour-long ride, and most of us stayed for the entire weekend.

There were always sixty or seventy people who attended. We had campfire gatherings, we hiked, sang, and danced. The trip was basically a bonding session, and we always ended our trip with a very memorable event.

On the last day of the retreat, we would gather in large circles with a big ball of yarn. Everyone would hold a piece of the yarn and reflect or share what this special moment meant to them before they passed it to the next member while still holding on to their small piece of the yarn. When we were done reflecting and the yarn had been passed around the entire group, everyone held onto a small piece.

The yarn reflected that we were all bonded by a single strand. We then cut the piece of the yarn that we held as a keepsake as part of a reminder of what it represented. It was really an emotional event.

I worked as an intern at the WXYZ-TV News 7 assignment desk during my sophomore semester at Wayne State University. They did a story on the newspaper strike and gave me a particular assignment to complete.

The Detroit News and Free Press were conducting interviews for scab workers to fill their vacant writing and editorial positions. My bosses at the station asked me if I would go undercover to seek employment at the Detroit Newspaper. I don't know why I was nervous, but I was and agreed to do it anyway. I thought this would be a terrific opportunity to impress the team and possibly get my internship extended.

They provided me with a bag that had a secret camera hidden inside. I thought the tiny lens was not small enough and voiced my concern. They assured me that the interviewer wouldn't notice the camera. I agreed and applied for the job. And wouldn't you know it, they called me and scheduled the interview.

When I arrived at the location, there was a very attractive woman who conducted the interview. She was voluptuous and exposed a lot of cleavage. She was extremely professional, but I questioned her attire. I remember she had on a form-fitting dress that accentuated every curve of her figure.

I placed the bag with the camera in the chair next to me as soon as I walked in. I made sure it aimed in the direction of her face. I prayed she didn't look at the bag too closely. I was still self-conscious about the size of that lens. She never noticed it and conducted the entire interview from the same seat. So, there was no need to adjust the angle. It was perfect.

When I returned to the station, the editors and news director crowded into the booth to see my video. I did it, and I was so proud to be a part of this team. I completed my first assignment.

When they played the video, all you could see were the woman's breasts the entire time. We talked for about thirty minutes. The whole time, the camera showed a tight shot of her neck and her cleavage. She never moved, save for adjusting her legs, so her cleavage bounced a bit. There were forty-five minutes of video of this woman's sultry voice and cleavage recorded. That's all I got. It was like an uncut scene from *The Graduate* with Dustin Hoffman.

All I could think of was, I failed that assignment miserably. What a waste of effort. The team had a good laugh and a free peep show. However, this video could not air on the show. I don't think they held it against me, though.

CHAPTER XXIII –
UNFORESEEN STRUGGLES

My junior and senior years at Wayne State were tough. Although I passed every class with a B average, I realized that this was not the community college that I had aced so easily. It became evident that I was not going to have last-minute preparations prior to exams and pass them with ease. I had to batten down the hatches and study like hell.

I called on Martha for more tutelage. If I wasn't going to lose this scholarship, I would have to study extra hard and ace all my tests.

I began to lean on my faith. I thought about my *dad, Judge Talbot, Gabe, Martha* … I couldn't let them down now.

Occasionally, if I wasn't prepared for a test, I'd make an excuse and take the test the following day. Most of my instructors were lenient and allowed it. I didn't do it often. I wasn't going to abuse this loophole.

One morning on test day, I just didn't want to take the test. I was prepared but simply not feeling it, and I knew I wouldn't get a great score feeling like I did. As I left the parking structure and walked towards the Matthaei Building where my class was, I suddenly felt anxiety and began making excuses to postpone the exam. My test phobia kicked in. I began procrastinating and slowed my pace across campus.

I knew I had come too far to make excuses. I convinced myself that my teacher would understand if I told her my car stalled and I couldn't make it to cIt was a lie, but I was hungry and I couldn't possibly pass a test on an empty stomach. Being hungry was a legitimate excuse for me to miss class today, so I turned around.

Because I had gone through so much to get back in school, my conscience bothered me about this decision to skip class.

I remember the day because it was sunny, clear, and calm. And just as I turned back and began to walk to my car, through the wide opening between the Student Center building and the Law School, a gust of wind from nowhere picked up slowly.

I could see something from about one hundred fifty yards away blowing like a candy wrapper in the wind. Oddly enough, it was flowing in my direction and hadn't changed its course. Therefore, I never took my eyes off it.

As it got closer, I still couldn't figure out what it was. When it got close enough, I recognized it–Just then, it hit my pant leg and stayed stuck there. It was a five-dollar bill—just enough to get the chicken sandwich and fries that I would get daily from a local bar on Cass Avenue for lunch between classes. I thought about the excuse I used to miss class and felt horrible.

I would love to tell you that I saw that incident as a sign and followed it ... went to the bar, ate, and satisfied my hunger, then passed that test. I went to the bar and ordered the chicken sandwich and fries. But unfortunately, I neglected that sign and went home afterwards.

I eventually retook the exam and aced it, but I let myself down by procrastinating. It was as though I intentionally and unnecessarily paused an event in my life. I let myself down at that moment, even though I made up for it later.

During my sophomore year, I got lucky. I was offered a full-time job as an assignment editor at WXYZ-TV News 7–the local ABC News station. I was geeked. There I was, thinking I would graduate from college with an English degree and begin publishing books. And now, I was getting a journalism degree and working for a top ten local news station. I watched this channel growing up and was now a part of that team. I was working alongside my local heroes.

I never knew they were hiring until three days prior to their decision. I applied when I found out at the last minute. I knew *John Dowaskin (the other intern)* had that job locked up. He was charismatic, bold, smart, and had an affluent background.

When they announced that the job was mine. I will never forget the look on *John's* face. He was beet red. I felt bad for him but was glad I got the job.

My getting the job may have been the best thing that happened to *John*, though. Years later, we invited him back as a guest. He became a young millionaire through some sort of investment company he formed. We hugged and laughed, and I never heard from him again.

At the assignment desk, I assisted with phones, faxes, and mail to catch and solicit stories. I really enjoyed it. I became pretty popular when I told them that my *Uncle Tomboy* was head of the homicide at the Detroit Police Department. Any newsworthy crimes that hit the scanner, I would be notified, and my station would report it first.

Boy, was I in for a shock. *Uncle Tomboy*, the same guy that interrogated me in my grandmother's basement years earlier, would go out of his way to notify my competitors and not notify me. I was shocked. I was so embarrassed that I called him about news tips he had purposely given to my competitors before notifying me. He said he didn't want to show favoritism.

I had friends running the assignment desks at WDIV 4 News and WJBK 2 News teasing me that my uncle was scooping them before me. They always called me to share the news he'd given them, but they made sure they had a head start before notifying me.

They were always on the scene first. So, from that point on, I avoided *Uncle Tomboy* altogether.

Detective *(Bill) Rice*, who was also a homicide investigator, knew that *Uncle Tomboy* was preventing me from beating my competitors.

106

He advised me that he would notify me immediately of any relevant homicides or other newsworthy stories that DPD were involved in. He was a man of his word. He began calling me and providing me with details on breaking stories. Suddenly, I was getting the scoops and beating the competitors. My team formed a disdain for *Uncle Tomboy,* and I completely understood and supported them.

I assumed he'd be proud of me for turning my life around, but he appeared to be purposely sabotaging my career. I came to trust *Bill Rice* completely. He became a trusted ally and a new best friend from that point on. I give Detective *Rice* credit for saving my reputation.

During my seven-year stint at Channel 7, I learned their system. I was working nights, so I helped out with sports a lot on the *Sports Final Edition* segment with *Don Shane.* My interns were mostly beautiful, educated young women with positive upsides. They always requested to assist me and ride to the stadiums with the photographers to interview athletes during games. I would send them to do the interview. It made my job easier with a shorthanded night crew and it really helped my sports team gather more material for the newscast.

But it seemed most were looking for a date more so than a story. My photographers would tell me that some of the young women I sent to cover the Pistons, Tigers, or Red Wings games dropped the tapes off to them and ended up catching a ride home with one of the players. It was crazy. These athletes had their pick of the litter when it came to beautiful young gold seekers. It was nuts.

I once got a firsthand view of what it was like to be a pro ballplayer during a Pistons game.

We had a game in which our media team played the mayor of Detroit's team in an exhibition basketball game. *Mayor Dennis Archer* put together a basketball team to play against local media members. It was billed as the Detroit media team against the city of Detroit employees. I quickly volunteered. The game was at the Palace of Auburn Hills. It took place immediately after the Utah Jazz played the

Detroit Pistons.

Of course, not even a quarter of the fans stayed to see us play. But hell, we had the Pistons' announcer, *Mason*, calling the game. It was great to be a celebrity athlete, even if it was only for four quarters.

We shared the dressing room with the *Pistons*. After halftime of their game with the Utah Jazz, we headed to the locker room to get dressed. The strategy was to come out immediately after the game, so all the fans didn't leave. When their game was over, we shared the locker room for a little while before heading out on the court to start our game.

It amazed me that so many women made it past security to line the tunnel. They looked handpicked. Most of the players' wives were well aware of these fame seekers, and they always attended these games to make sure their husbands stuck to the routine: get showered, dressed, and go home.

The rookies had a ball. Jerome Williams, aka *Junk Yard Dog*, had a woman under each arm. It was hilarious. I figured that the first few years for a single rookie pro athlete had to be the toughest for them if they were in a relationship.

I did Sports Edition after the 11 o'clock news on Sundays, and I got really cool with *Joe Dumars*. He was the designated *Piston* to join *Don Shane* on Sunday nights. He was always my favorite *Bad Boy* member. He was a class act.

I enjoyed chatting away with him on Sunday nights. When he walked in to tape the sports segment, he always greeted me like I'd just scored a basket during a game. He and *John Salley* were the coolest *Piston* players I ever met.

During my stint at Channel 7, the Wings won the Stanley Cup, and I met *Steve Yzerman*. I had seen him come into the station for years and had no idea who he was. He looked dignified and wore a long overcoat. I was surprised he was missing a front tooth. I thought he looked like a mobster of sorts with a flaw (the missing tooth). But then, when the Wings won the Stanley Cup in 1997, and we stood in a circle to drink from the Stanley Cup, he was first to drink and had the biggest smile on his face. I asked *Diana* (Ladi Di) who he was, and she looked at me in shock and said, ***"That's Stevie Yzerman."*** That explained the missing tooth. We passed the cup around and merrily drank the champagne.

I graduated the year the Wings won that championship. I was honored. Of all my siblings, I was the first of us with a four-year college degree. Hell, I had two degrees: an associate's and a bachelor's degree.

My mom was so proud. Channel 7 was just as proud. They covered my graduation as a closer on the late-night news segment. I was honored. There I was, walking across the stage with my cap and gown, and it was being televised on our local news station—a top ten local news station, at that.

People recognized me. My life had come full circle.

The station's general manager always spoke to me. Her name was *Grace Gilchrist*. She was a wonderful woman. I will never forget her. She was so sweet and occasionally asked me what I wanted to do at the station. I was unsure but knew I wanted to be a part of the nucleus. Being an assignment editor and a writer was fun for me. I was writing voice-overs, finding stories, pairing photographers with reporters, then guiding them to the stories. I advised her that I was content with what I was doing for now.

I would always visit the control booth during the newscast. I loved to see the engineers making all the pieces come together for the show. Everything was in place, and the show was ready to begin. After the show, the engineers would ask me to sit at the anchor desk and read

the teleprompter. I did it, and that's when I realized that I was not cut out to be in front of the camera—at least not for now.

The funny thing is, during my college days I performed poetry around the city of Detroit during the poetry slams. I really enjoyed performing at Stuart's and Union Street restaurants. But, for some reason, I was not comfortable at that news desk. Maybe it was because I knew that a million or so people could be watching.

Nevertheless, either the general manager, news director, or someone else would constantly ask me what else I wanted to do at the station. I was still content as an assignment editor. I was part of the nucleus of the place. I didn't determine the order of stories and didn't even have a guarantee that all the ones I chased down would air. However, I felt that this position made me a vital part of the team.

I believed my team wanted me to be an on-air talent because I was suddenly asked to grab a photographer, head out and shoot any story I wanted to shoot. They suggested it be a human-interest story.

I was given four hours to complete the story. Me, being from the streets of Detroit, knew just the story. I knew an attorney who was married to a judge. The attorney was known for defending high profile drug dealers and caught a lot of heat for it. I knew about him from my street days. I wanted to get his take on all the bribery, extortion, and other accusations levied against him. I thought this would be a great story, so I pursued it.

My first stop was the public defenders' office. They were welcoming. They let me in and offered me coffee. The minute I asked them about the attorney, they immediately asked what the story was about. I said it was just an exposé I was doing on the attorney and wanted insights from those who knew him.

They immediately said, *"No comment."* I thought, what? So, I tried the prosecutor's office. I was hit with, *"No comment"* as soon as they learned who the story was about.

So, I turned to my sources at the Detroit police department. I had two first cousins who worked in narcotics, a useless aunt who worked the desk at 1300 Beaubien—*Uncle Tomboy's* sister—and my new best friend, *Bill Rice*.

I turned to *Bill*. I knew *Uncle Tomboy* was out of the question.

This guy was my uncle. And he gave my competitors the stories instead of me. He retired from the police department and became chief investigator at the Wayne County morgue and would confirm death notices to my competitors prior to talking to me. Then he worked as head of security for the Detroit Lions and never offered me a ticket, but he offered them to my family members, even *Old Man*. He sucked, and I could never rely on him.

Bill Rice was my new source and my best bet. I went to his office and talked to him about my story.

He looked at me with an air of concern, lowered his eyes, and said in a low tone, **"You're barking up the wrong tree."** Then he continued, **"Leave that guy alone."**

His veiled warning frightened me. I dropped the story after I had spent three hours chasing it. *Bill* said I had no business putting that story together. He advised me that the attorney was a guy I didn't want to deal with.

Now, I only had an hour to come up with a story and get back to the station. I went back with a freeway traffic voice-over. I found a huge pothole that backed up rush hour traffic on the southbound Southfield Freeway. I don't even think the story aired.

The second story I was asked to cover was to simply grab soundbites from Governor John Engler—easy enough. I figured I would just wait on seasoned reporters to ask the tough questions and have my photographer video while I squeezed through the throng of reporters and positioned my microphone close enough to get a good response to the questions asked by the reporter.

111

We got there and things were set up according to plan. But then Governor Engler told his press secretary that he'd only field questions from one reporter. Everyone else could observe and record. He surveyed the sea of reporters and pointed me out! I wanted to scream, "Why me!" But I knew why. He had never seen me before and assumed correctly—that I was a rookie with no hard-hitting question experience. I wasn't prepared to ask about his controversial environmental deregulations' laws, welfare and education reforms, or his desires to privatize public services.

Instead, I was like a deer caught in the headlights at that moment. This further solidified my reasoning to stay off that anchor desk—I was not ready for this shit. I asked a few dull questions. He got out of that press conference unscathed, and I was his scapegoat.

The third story was another full circle moment for me. I was headed back to Lansing, Michigan to cover a circuit court judge who was running for a Michigan Supreme Court seat. I didn't have an available reporter, so the news manager insisted I go. I wasn't really prepared for the two-hour ride, but the story was needed for the 6 p.m. newscast. As long as it wasn't John Engler again, I was good. Besides, if I decided to be a reporter, this was experience under my belt. After all, I did have a journalism degree and was headed to Lansing for another interview with another promising Michigander.

We got there early. There were a few photographers and reporters, but they hadn't set up. My photographer spotted the judge looking calmly out of the window. He asked the judge where he would like for him to set up. I was preoccupied, talking to another reporter, trying to get some good question ideas. When I turned around, the judge and I locked eyes from a distance.

Suddenly, he looked extremely surprised and very serious at me. Then he took off his glasses, as if to get a clearer view. I was walking toward him, trying to be professional, but the nearer I got, the more emotional I became. When I reached him, I couldn't hold up. I hugged him and cried. Tears welled in his eyes as well.

We must have embraced for two minutes or so. We talked in low whispers. I thanked him for believing in me years earlier, and for sparing my life and allowing me another opportunity at life. He thanked me for proving him right and making the best of my opportunity.

Now, I was before Judge Michael Talbot again. But this time, outside of a courtroom setting. It was great. Judging from the smile on his face, I made his day. And he made mine.

For years, I wanted to make this man proud of me for believing in me and allowing me to turn my life around. And now I was living proof of what we had achieved. The moment was truly priceless.

The interview went great. My photographer was satisfied, and we wrapped up. The judge and I embraced one last time. I promised him that I would keep pushing to make him proud. He told me that I had already done that.

As we packed up and began to leave, I looked back and broke protocol again. I yelled, *"Judge Michael Talbot, you are not just a judge running for a Supreme Court seat; you're a wonderful and caring human being as well. And you certainly have my vote."*

On the ride home, I knew what my photographer was thinking: How did I know this conservative, white, circuit court judge so well? And my thoughts were confirmed when he asked me.

I couldn't look at him when I responded. My eyes were welling up with water again. But I simply responded, *"Me and the judge go way back. I know him from downtown Detroit."*

I was having a moment during the ride back—staring out the window, waiting to get back to put my story together.

CHAPTER XXIV –
MAKING THE MOST OF IT

When there were no breaking stories, I could relax before the 11 o'clock newscast. My work was done. I could either hang out in the control booth with the engineers or in the sports department and watch the show. All the videos and soundbites were edited, double-checked, and queued up. Reporters were at their live locations.

After the show, I occasionally went to McVee's Bar and Grill with *Reggie*, the sports producer. We'd gotten closer because he always asked me if I could spare an intern to cover sporting events. I always spared an intern for him and *Don Shane*.

Reggie and *John Salley* were cool. He would share pictures of them sitting in old classic vehicles. He even introduced me to *John Salley* once. *Salley* was another one of my favorite Bad Boys, so I was excited to meet him. I liked him and thought he was funny. He should have been a comedian.

Reggie graduated from the University of Detroit and would always cover and attend their basketball games. He talked about the Titans all the time, as if they were on the verge of winning the National Championship.

He never missed their home games. You always saw *Reggie* in the highlight reels, sitting in the same spot in the bleachers, yelling and cheering them on.

Years later, I heard about an accident on northbound John C. Lodge. The car hit the median and rolled over. The driver was killed instantly. I later learned it was *Reggie*. I was sickened. *Reggie* loved life as much as anyone I knew. He lived for sports and loved the University of Detroit basketball.

I was told that in *Reggie's* honor, the school renamed a section of the bleachers where he once cheered on his Titans.

I went to McVee's Bar and Grill after his death and saw *Reggie's* picture hanging behind the bar. I toasted to his image in honor of our friendship.

One of the most beautiful interns I'd ever seen was from Florida but attended Michigan State University. I designated her to the sports department. She owned a tanning salon back home that was pretty successful. She told me she was planning on opening more of them in Michigan with the help of her parents. I understood her business approach, especially with the finances from her parents to open more spas, but I questioned her true passion for journalism. I got the impression from her response that she wanted nothing to do with journalism and was just satisfying her parents' wishes of simply going away to college. She appeared beautiful and bored in this fast-paced environment.

However, we discussed the possibility of her pursuing a business degree as well. She contemplated changing her major. Business studies for her made sense to me. I would send her to cover Pistons and Tigers games, and she always came back on time with the tapes. She never seemed infatuated with the players like the other interns. She sometimes turned down sports stories to cover human-interest stories. I liked her and thought she was very down-to-earth.

She and her best friend once asked me to come to Lansing to attend a party. My blood pressure shot up. Me? —I thought. But I made an excuse about the drive being too far for me to be drinking and getting on the highway coming back from Lansing going to Detroit. They both excitedly said, **"You could stay with us until the next day if the driving is an issue."**

It was like a dream come true. Beautiful college "Girls Gone Wild" wanted me to have drinks with them and spend the night with them. I was shocked. But I resisted.

From where I came from, the excitement for me was not sacrificing my position for these college beauties, but finishing what I started. I could not risk it. As beautiful and as sexy as they were, I had a long way to go. I could not be derailed by sex. However, I wondered if she was just looking for a fun time or if she really liked me. Because if she really liked me, it may have been worth the trip. She could have been Mrs. Snell.

I really liked one intern from the start. He was serious about his craft. He was the youngest but knew what he wanted when he walked in the door. He was extremely talented. He wanted to be a news anchor

and told me that he once appeared on *The Phil Donahue* Show as a fifteen year old. He was discussing his concerns about the environment. I didn't believe him until I looked it up. There he was, sitting on the panel as a guest with *Phil*, talking to him and his mom. At fifteen years old, he looked very poised.

His name was *Roop Raj*, I thought *Roop* would make a great reporter. He would bring back the greatest sound bites, and you could hear him asking the questions on the video. He never relied on seasoned reporters to ask questions to get his sound bites. He always took the initiative.

I was saddened when he would come to me feeling melancholy because some jerk reporter would criticize and discourage him. He appeared to begin questioning his own talents and drive. I explained to him that he was an intern and that if the veterans were criticizing him, and it wasn't constructive criticism, then they were concerned that his talents might overshadow their own one day. I told him that it sounded like jealousy. We laughed, and his confidence always shot through the roof again after all of our discussions. I was determined to keep his spirits up.

I assured him that I, of all people, knew what he was going through. I comforted him every time he came to me. I was convinced—and convinced him—that his talents would not be wasted. I assured him that

116

it is people's job to try to try to discourage him when he's capable of greatness. And that it was his job to prove he was worthy of that greatness.

I loved this kid, *Roop Raj*, and promised him one day he would sit at an anchor's desk and read the news nightly. His dream and my wish had come true. I saw him after he had become a local celebrity as a Fox 2 News anchor. We smiled and hugged.

Years later, when I worked for a nonprofit organization, I was asked to find an M.C. to host an event for Red Wings owner *Mike Ilitch's* wife, *Marian Ilitch*. She was presented with an award for her community involvement and philanthropy.

The group asked if I could get *Emery King* to host the event because they knew that I worked with *Emery* at Channel 4 News in Detroit at the time. I promised them I would try to make that happen. *Emery* was golfing in Florida, so I hatched my alternative plan.

I immediately called *Roop* and asked him if he would be available on that day to host the event. He informed me that FOX 2 had to clear it first. I provided them with all the details, and they approved. Deep down, I wanted *Roop* to do it anyway. He was young and I wanted him to establish himself in Detroit.

At the eleventh hour, I informed the team that *Emery* was still in Florida at a golfing event and wouldn't make it back in time so he wouldn't be able to host the event.

But I informed them that *Roop Raj* was available and willing to host it. It was too late to change now. *Roop* was our man.

I think the committee members were disappointed when *Roop*, and not *Emery*, hosted the event, but I loved it. He performed great—*Roop Raj* had arrived.

CHAPTER XXV –
TRUE TALENT

Everything was fast-paced around the newsroom. It was still amazing working there. I was hanging out with the talent a lot. The most gifted talent I'd ever met was *Frank Turner.* He came across as arrogant as hell, but when I got to know him, I was shocked at how down-to-earth he was. I picked his brain and really got to know him. I watched him from the control booth during the newscast when he anchored the show, because I had written many of his scripts.

I paid particular attention to see how much he ad-libbed my material. He was so talented that when a script had an error on the teleprompter, you rarely heard it on air. *Frank* would catch the errors as he read the teleprompter and verbally change them on air. The passage made perfect sense to the audience, and he never delayed or paused to indicate the error or the last minute changes he'd made to the script.

He was like *Peyton Manning* performing audibles at the line of scrimmage. He'd change the play impromptu and score a touchdown. The audience would think the winning play was designed from the start.

Diana Lewis (Lady Di) was great, too. She'd gotten so comfortable with me prior to her 11 o'clock show that we began eating lunch together nearly every day. We made a pact: whoever flew, the other would buy. Needless to say, I always flew. At that point, I think she was one of the very few local anchors making a million dollars annually—or close to it. I was still getting beginner's pay. I ate corned beef nearly every night with her. That's what she liked, and who was I to argue? Besides, I liked corned beef as well.

She once set me up on a date with one of the writers. She had known this girl for years and thought we'd really hit it off. I hesitated because of a piece of advice that someone gave me long before I got there. "Don't shit where you sleep," they advised me. That cliché meant nothing to me at the time. Besides, *Lady Di* wouldn't steer me wrong— or so I thought.

I turned down a couple of advances from very popular women who anchored the news.

Not solely because I respected them too much, but I didn't trust them. I kindly told them that I'd been watching them for so long and that I had too much respect for them to carry on a fling.

One woman, making one of the largest salaries, even offered to put me up in a condo and buy me a car. I politely explained to her that if I accepted the car and condo, I wouldn't respect myself for taking them, but I thanked her.

Now, here I was, contemplating a date with this woman and ignoring the earlier advice given to me about not dating coworkers. But I was single and *Ladi Di* implored, so I went against my better judgement and considered the date anyway. The woman wasn't "million-dollar" talent, so I hoped that would make it easier for me to connect on a more genuine level.

She was extremely sweet and always smiled when I would catch her looking at me. So, after a few days, *Lady Di* asked if I had made up my mind. I accepted and decided to take the woman on a date.

The date started off great. We had gone to lunch, and she called me later that night. We talked for about an hour. I deduced from her conversation that she was a bit sheltered growing up. But that was okay. To me, that reflected an innocence about her.

I was still a little hesitant about the second date. What triggered my concerns was that she wanted to cook me dinner. That meant I had to visit her house and would probably be there later than I wanted to be. I kept *Lady Di* in the loop so she would know about my intentions, and nothing could be misconstrued.

Dinner was great. Afterwards, she wanted to watch a movie. I agreed to watch the movie. I think the movie was An *Unfinished Affair* with Faith Ford.

Suddenly, it was as if her innocence had abandoned her. She slid her thigh across my leg as we sat on the couch watching the movie. I was shocked.

I wasn't new or naïve to this sort of reaction from women. But this was a coworker, and I had to be very careful—especially now. I suddenly began questioning her intentions in my mind. This naïve girl had suddenly exploded out of an airtight shell and was trying to seduce

the hell out of me. She began taking my hand and rubbing it over her breast.

Had this not been a coworker, but a regular date, I might have explored that body like *Jacques Cousteau* explored the oceans, but I resisted.

After the movie, she offered more wine, and I refused and complained about my early morning appointment.

She asked me out again, and I accepted a lunch invitation only. My intentions were to let her know that I appreciated the date but wasn't ready for anything serious. I sensed that she was fragile, so I had to be careful in my approach. It was my responsibility to keep her dignity intact. After all, I had agreed to the date in the first place.

During lunch, I explained that she was a very beautiful girl, inside and out, but that I wasn't ready for a relationship at this time and didn't want to feel that I was taking advantage of her in any way. I thought the letdown went well. She had worked as a writer at the station for ten years and I was just starting out, so I did not want there to be any hard feelings.

When we got back to work the next day, she rolled her eyes at me every time I looked in her direction. I went over to her cubicle and asked if everything was okay. She didn't say a word. Here I was, the only nontalent minority male on this newsroom floor being shunned by the most innocent angel to ever sully the walkways of the Channel 7 newsroom. I was devastated and desperate to repair this damaged friendship between us.

*Lady D*i came to me asking what happened. I explained everything and said there were no hard feelings when I left. She then asked if I had slept with her. I thought it was none of her business but answered, **"No."** I was honest. I begged *Lady Di* to talk to her.

For the next two months, I would come in to work, speak, and she never acknowledged me. I was nervous. My background would not afford me the benefit of the doubt in this situation - I was cooked. This girl was bringing me down with false perceptions. Only she could stop it, and she was unwilling. The next thing I knew, she was visiting *Lady Di's* dressing room, teary-eyed, seeking compassion prior to the newscast. No more "I fly, you buy" shit for me.

Even *Lady Di* was shunning me.

Then it all came together. I felt the whole matchmaking deal was a deflection from my earlier response to a sugar momma letdown. I choose not to elaborate any further on the passage in order to protect her identity.

I had had enough and just said, Fuck it! I know who I am and I had shown that woman nothing but respect. If she wanted to play that game and give people a false impression of me, then shame on her. She can have at it, I decided. No more apologies from me.

From then on, I came in and concentrated on my work. Others looked at me, but never mentioned anything about the girl's silent attitude towards me. I assumed they knew what was going on because of her sudden reactions to me. She let it be known that she despised me after our dates.

The impression was already there, and I knew what people were thinking: "This horny son of a bitch corrupted our angel."

But at that point, I really didn't care what they believed. Only she and I knew what really happened, and she was unwilling to tell the truth.

Months went by, and I still hadn't spoken to her, and I had very little to say to *Lady Di* as well. I stayed respectful, though. "What's done is done," I thought. Those who had their impressions of me had them because of a lie or simply because they wanted to view me that way. Whatever repercussions I was going to face at the station, so be it.

Suddenly, after three or four months, the girl walked up to me after the newscast and apologized. I looked for sincerity. I could not afford to be set up again. I told her that I accepted her apology. But she kept talking. She admitted that she was wrong to feel the way she felt about me. It was as though she was attempting to restore my reputation.

She was admitting this in front of anyone who was there. She even said she reacted that way because she liked me so much.

Then she stood there, cried, and said I must hate her. I got up from my chair and hugged her, then told her that nothing she could have done would make me hate her.

She held me tighter and sobbed profusely.

To this day, when I see her, we hug as if we were lost souls finding each other—but I have no intentions of rekindling anything. I loved her for finally admitting the truth the way she did, though.

I often wonder if she ever got married or had kids. I'm sure she would have made a good mother.

CHAPTER XXVI –
AN UNWELCOMED GOOD CHANGE

My goal was to try to change the world. I was part of an organization that presented news and allowed people to shape their own perceptions of things. I found stories in the city and wrote them. I worked nights, so there was little resistance from managers and producers to air the stories I presented.

The closures were always cute and heartwarming stories that ended the newscast.

These were considered the recency effect stories—the *feel-good* stories that we hoped had a lasting impression on you (the viewer). These stories left you with a warm feeling and would, hopefully, have you tune in to the next newscast.

Christy McDonald was the producer, and I was the assignment editor on the night crew.

I thought she was as talented as any producer I had ever worked with. She kind of reminded me of a suburbanite who knew of Detroit but didn't actually know the city. I had grown up in the city and had ran those streets most of my life, so I was very familiar with Detroit.

I thought her story selections regarding Detroit were too crime-ridden. So, when I heard about a group of Detroit elementary school kids beautifying their school by planting gardens and flowers on school grounds. I had a photographer shoot it. Occasionally, I was asked to find a closure story because the producers were too busy. This time, the story fell right into my lap. It was a beautiful, heartwarming story. I approached *Christy* with the story and advised her that this would be a great closer for the night. She agreed.

Prior to the newscast, I viewed her lineup and saw a different closer. This closer was about white kids from a suburban school cleaning up their neighborhood. They were picking up paper from their local streets and parks. I was livid that she had a photographer go and shoot this piece and not advise me. It replaced the story she and I had agreed upon just two hours earlier. After the newscast, we argued. I had the worst impression of her and accused her of purposely airing

so much negativity about Detroit and ignoring the good that the city had to offer. I questioned why both stories could not air. She complained about the allotted time and advised me that only one story could make the show.

I had always had this opinion about her views of Detroit, but I kept it bottled up. This time, however, I let her have it. During our face-off, someone called the news director. I remember telling him about the situation, and he understood, but said she aired what she saw fit for her newscast. At that moment, I remember thinking to myself, how can I make a difference if I couldn't get a producer to air my story?

My approach had to be different. I had to join a like-minded producer's team. However, I was in no position to select who I worked with. *Mickey* controlled the assignment desk during the day shift and had it on lockdown. He worked with all my favorite producers. I wasn't getting his spot.

I thought that if I could select and edit stories, I could have more influence in my craft.

But here, the unions were so strong that I couldn't touch the editing machines if I didn't belong to the union.

Then suddenly, a sort of divine intervention happened. I was being offered a new job, pretty much without my knowledge. ABC News 12 in Flint, Michigan, wanted me. I did not want to go to fuckin' Flint. I had never been there but knew I didn't want to live or work there.

Everyone was treating me as if this was a wonderful transition and a celebratory moment. They told me that the Flint station was an ABC-owned station and that I would be allowed to work on the editing machines.

They convinced me that this was a good opportunity. So, I made up my mind and was Flint bound. I wanted to edit, but I didn't want to be pigeonholed as an editor, and I needed to find my calling. I concluded that this was a part of my life's journey.

I had seen a few anchors and major talents move on. And by now, I'd been at Channel 7 for seven years. I guessed it was my time to move on.

The station always had two types of send-offs. For anchors and long tenured reporters, there was always a Channel 7 cake with the station's design on it and a soirée to see them off. Everyone else got signed cards and was taken to lunch by a few team members.

As you can imagine, there were a lot of whispers when it was time for me to leave. I got the cake and a soirée that was usually reserved for news anchors and reporters. The celebration took place immediately after the 6 p.m. newscast, so everyone was there.

This made my departure somewhat tolerable. I wanted to stay here forever, or at least until I figured out what I wanted to do with myself. But it was time for me to go. Being there had its ups and downs, but I loved it. It was a wonderful experience.

I formed great bonds with the other assignment desk editors from other stations in Detroit throughout the years. *Bill Mullen* and *James Jackson* were my competitive companions.

We stayed connected over the years. They were the greatest co-workers, competitors, and friends that anyone could ever have. They taught me so much over the years.

Thank you both!

CHAPTER XXVII –
GETTING ACCLIMATED TO MY
NEW SURROUNDINGS

WJRT News 12 was a new journey for me. I edited a lot of stories, and the guys in charge, *Jim Bleicher* and *Phil Hendrix*, were two of the greatest guys in the business.

They welcomed me with open arms and assisted me with anything I needed. They both helped me tremendously in honing my craft. However, their approach to news was vastly different from what I was used to.

They covered high school basketball as though it was the NBA. It was shocking. I had never covered high school games. In Detroit, a few stations occasionally had a sports blurb regarding high school league or state championships.

But covering high school basketball games was a priority here. I had little interest in covering high school sports, but had to cover every game from all angles. And I always had to reserve a crew to cover the games. Their fascination for the sport made me curious, so I decided to go to one of the games.

I realized that a lot of the players were from the surrounding Saginaw-Flint area, and many of them made their way to the pros via Michigan State University. I'm sure other colleges benefitted from recruiting these talented area kids as well, but MSU was the pitstop for most.

I personally did not see how they made it. The pressure that these news crews put on these kids was unheard of. They were treated as celebrities before getting out of high school by the local media. These kids were signing autographs for hours after a game, and fans never left until the players left. It was interesting.

The Mayor of Flint, *Mayor Stanley*, likened himself to Mayor Coleman A. Young in Detroit. As you can imagine, that wasn't very popular among some of the nonblack residents and businessmen in the city. I saw that he lacked Mayor Young's tactless approach to the media. That was probably a good thing. Nevertheless, he had his work cut out for him.

He once held a press conference about a mundane wage increase regarding a local business on the verge of a strike, and a reporter yelled out, ***"What about GM's announcement regarding their truck assembly plant?"*** Apparently, GM was making a major move to cut more jobs from an already depleted workforce previously decreased from recent layoffs. They announced plans to cut thousands of more jobs by 2006.

Mayor Stanley knew nothing about the GM announcement. He wasn't made aware of what was happening in his own backyard. It appeared he was purposely kept in the dark regarding that issue. When the question was posed, he was like a deer caught in the headlights.

I had gotten really cool with the mayor's press secretary. She would sometimes ask me to go to lunch. I initially joined her to stay in their good graces for any interviews that I might need down the line. Besides, she was a nice woman, and I enjoyed her company.

This GM thing was a real problem for them. She spoke of how stupid he looked during that press conference and asked me what I thought.

I didn't want to poison my well, but I gave my opinion nonetheless. She casually continued her salad while waiting for a response. I recalled saying, in a joking manner, ***"Take the Coleman Young picture down in his office and have him put it up in his home instead."***

I didn't know how she'd respond, but she laughed and said,

"Maybe you're right." I quickly changed the subject.

Mayor Stanley served as Flint mayor from 1991 until 2002. A recall that ousted him in 2002 ended his reign as mayor. He died in 2022. I remembered him as an immensely proud man.

I was tested my first week on the job. One of the most beautiful reporters sat on my assignment desk, eating an ice cream cone, seductively. She was directly in front of me, asking me who I was and where I was from.

Her cleavage in clear view, long beautiful legs dangled from the desk, and she was constantly flipping beautiful almond hair from one side to the other as if there was a breeze flowing through the office.

I asked her politely, **"How can I concentrate on what you are asking me with you in my** *personal* **space this way?"**

She seemed flabbergasted at my reply, but then she sensed the seriousness of my mood and got down. I don't think she was interested in a response to her questions. I got the impression that she was just trying to throw me off my game. I could see in her face that she was shocked that I had ignored her seductiveness the way I did.

Had she shown up at my apartment in Grand Blanc, just ten minutes outside the city, I probably would have lifted her from my desk, gone in for a kiss, and found out if her intentions were real. If so, she could have been another Mrs. Snell as well. She was gorgeous.

One day, *Jim, Phil,* and the lead anchor called me into *Bleicher's* office. They wanted to know what I thought about them bringing *Glenda Lewis* in as a reporter. This was *Lady Di's* youngest daughter, and she had started interning at WXYZ Channel 7 before I left. So we worked together briefly.

We'd gotten to know each other, and I thought she was beautiful. She'd even invited me to her house party when I was at WXYZ Channel 7. Even though I rarely attended parties, I thought it was great that she invited me. And to be courteous, I accepted the invitation.

I'd heard her mom had a mansion in a nearby suburb, so I figured about ten to twenty people would show up for the party. I imagined a pretty intimate bunch. When I got there, I was amazed. I thought, "Holy shit! Now this is a party." About a hundred MSU students showed up, and I didn't know any of them. DMX's Ruff Ryders' Anthem blared from the speakers, and everyone was in chorus screaming the lyrics. I was like a fish out of water. I drank a beer or two and left. If it got rowdy, I didn't want any part of it. But I enjoyed about an hour of the festivities before I left.

I loved *Glenda*, but my journey was different. I didn't care if I was never invited to another one of her parties, but I thought she was great for inviting me.

I told *Jim* and *Phil* that she was a wonderful person, and I would be ecstatic about working with her again.

We caught up on old times when she arrived in Flint. She relished the opportunity to hone her reporting and anchor skills, then getting

back to the larger market. We both loved clams and usually hit a local bar after work. One of the bars had some of the best clams in the city. I think of how we ate mussels and clams out of a bucket, breaking the shells and devouring them together. We never cared how we looked afterward and always laughed about it.

I liked her more and more as time went on. I think of how down-to-earth she was about everything. I often wondered what could have been if we had continued to spend more time together.

About a year or so later, she returned to Detroit to fill her mom's shoes. She now reports and anchors the local news from the same seat her mom sat. She looks just like her as well. I enjoyed our time together.

Once, I was asked if I could cover a Lions game. It was a far cry from the high school sports I had grown accustomed to covering in Flint.

The Lions hosted the Monday Night Football game at the Pontiac Silverdome. I hated being in the middle of sports crowds, but I agreed to go.

I had a press pass, and my photographer showed me where the best location was to secure the interviews after the game. I told him that I would meet him there just before the game was over, and we would talk to some of the standout players of the night.

As I walked around, I spoke to *Dan Dierdorf* and *Al Michaels*. They shook my hand and asked me what station I was from. I told them ABC Flint and mentioned that I didn't want to be on the field because I couldn't really view the game from there. They invited me into their booth where they were calling the game's play-by-play. It was great. In their suite, I had the option to view the game on the monitor or look down on the field. This was exactly where I wanted to be. I sat there quietly and observed while they called the game.

Everything was going through my head. How could I prove that I was actually here during Monday Night Football with these two sports titans? I was observing and judging their play-by-play skills.

I thought, if I knocked that camera over during their live shot and we blacked out, I'd have caused that delay, and everyone would know it was me in that booth. But I abandoned that wicked fantasy quickly.

Prior to the game's end, I thanked the guys, hugged them, and left for the field to meet my photographer. Everything went great.

I found *Barry Sanders*, chatted about his amazing 47-yard burst that ignited the crowd, and headed back to the station.

About a month later, I was summoned back to the office. It turns out *Jim* and *Phil* wanted my opinion again. They mentioned to me that they were thinking about bringing someone in as a producer and wanted to know what I thought about them. It turns out, I worked with this producer. It was *Christy McDonald*.

We had history! This was the same woman that I judged as out of touch with the city when she rejected my closing story back in Detroit. I was at a loss for words. I didn't care if I never saw her again. And now, here she was, basically at my mercy. Her fate was determined by my denial or approval of her being here.

I don't know what they saw on my face, but what came out of my mouth was, ***"She'll probably be one of the best producers you'll ever hire. She is a great writer as well,"*** I continued. ***"As a matter of fact, you will get the best of both worlds in hiring her."***

They both looked respectfully at me and asked what I thought about her personally.

I thought about it, then laughed and said, ***"My personal opinion shouldn't matter. I can tell you that we've worked well together in the past. And we will work through any obstacles at this stage of our careers."*** I assured them that *Glenda, Christy,* and I, for the most part, worked well together in Detroit and would do so here.

They then asked me another question. They wanted to know that if I were in their position, would I hire her? I didn't hesitate in my response. ***"Absolutely,"*** I continued. ***"As a matter of fact, if I were you, I'd hire her before someone else does."*** They did.

Here I was, singing the praises of the very woman who sabotaged my closing story years earlier. But her talents were undeniable, and she deserved her success. She went on to host her own talk show and did very well.

I did well in Flint. I edited stories, created a lot of voice-overs, and collected a lot of soundbites. It was weird rushing into the booths to beat deadlines, but I was doing it well. At ABC in Detroit, I couldn't touch those machines, and now I had mastered them.

One day, I got a call on the station's hotline. *Jim's* assistant excitedly interrupted our morning meeting to announce that I had a call. She continued, in front of everyone, to tell me that *Asha Blake* was on the line for me. *Asha* was a very attractive reporter and weekend anchor at WDIV Channel 4 in Detroit who ended up doing national news on the Later Today show.

I met her at an event in Detroit. We chatted about working in Detroit and then exchanged numbers.

When I met her, she and I briefly discussed stories and shared ideas in a very short conversation. Then we exchanged phone numbers before she was summoned back to the station. I didn't even think she'd remember me—let alone call me.

Phil and *Jim* walked into the office where I took the call and sat down. They were dying to hear my conversation with *Asha*. I was so embarrassed that I held the phone, put my hand over the receiver, and looked at them as if to say, "Please allow me some privacy," but they didn't and I thought this was so disrespectful. But I'm sure they were eager to know what this extremely attractive woman wanted with me.

I simply told her I was pleased that she remembered me and that I was glad she called.

I informed her that I was in the middle of an assignment and would call her back when I got the chance. Then we said our goodbyes. The guys seemed disappointed that that was all they got to hear.

I never really followed up with *Asha* but I wondered if she would have went on a lunch date with me if I had asked her. I guess I'll never know.

Nevertheless, *Jim* and *Phil* became my friends. I loved their attitudes and learned a lot from them. They taught me everything they could, and I was grateful for it.

When I left, it was devastating. But my journey was far from over.

A representative from WDIV Channel 4 News called me. I remember when I picked up the line, I clearly recall them asking, ***"Are you ready to come home? We have an assignment desk position for you here if you're interested."*** I nearly fell out of my chair with excitement, but I kept my composure and said, ***"Yes, I am."***

I gave the station three weeks' notice and prepped for my new gig. Then they called back and asked if I knew anyone who could fill a producer's role starting at $85,000.

I knew just the person—*Phil*. Although I did not want to break up that duo, I had to let him know. He was only getting about sixty to seventy thousand dollars in Flint. I thought this would be an upgrade from where he was and what he earned. Besides, I'd worked with him and would relish the opportunity to work with him again in the big city. I knew he would go for it, and he did—hook, line, and sinker.

Four days before I was scheduled to start my new job, they scheduled *Phil's* interview. I told him how excited I was to have the opportunity to work with him again in the big city.

I advised him that I would support him in any way possible. I promised to show him around and show him the ins and outs of Detroit. He seemed ecstatic to be heading to the big market, and I was excited to be going back as well.

Two days later, my phone rang again. I knew the number. It was Channel 4. I immediately answered, and they asked me if I had heard from Phil. His interview was in fifteen minutes, and he wasn't answering his phone. I assured them that he was a very responsible guy and that I would get in touch with him and have him return their call immediately.

He didn't answer the phone for me either. I called about fifteen times straight. None of the stations had reported any accidents on I-75 between Flint and Downtown Detroit.

So, I assumed he was safe. Maybe he was just running late. I called the station back.

He was late for the interview at this point and still hadn't called.

After another hour, Phil finally called me back. I was expecting an accident or some sort of emergency story. But he simply said, "I can't take the job."

I thought he was kidding—this had to be a joke. It turns out he got cold feet and didn't think he could handle the big market. I angrily asked why he hadn't called them to cancel the interview. He assured me that he would do it right away.

I was livid. My reputation had taken a severe blow before I even started at WDIV Channel 4 News. I vouched for this guy. I was supposed to be the best man at his wedding, and he did this. I never knew he was capable of this. Not *Phil*. But yes, it was *Phil*, and he was capable.

Ironically, *Carolyn Clifford* was the best wo/man at his wedding. I wasn't shocked about her taking my place. It appeared he was used to doing an about-face on his commitments.

At this point, I wasn't eager to be at his wedding anyway. I loved *Nikki* (his wife), but the guy she was marrying really let me down, and she had to know it. I was sure she would understand my decision to bow out of attending the wedding. Ironically, *Carolyn Clifford* later became a WDIV Channel 4 anchor who filled in for *Carmen Harlan* after her retirement. This was the very station he stood up.

CHAPTER XXVIII –
LET THE GAMES BEGIN

WDIV Channel 4 was in the heart of Detroit. And 1300 Beaubien (Detroit Police Headquarters) was nearby, so my cop connections were at my fingertips. I knew the city like the back of my hand and would be first on the scene of any newsworthy stories.

Besides, I was working with *James Jackson*, my former competitor who used to beat me on local stories when I was at WXYZ Channel 7. He knew the city as well as I,

He was great. We were going to become a trusted tandem on that assignment desk. He consoled me about *Phil's* "no-show" antics and told me to forget about it. He reassured me that it wasn't my fault. So, I tried to forget about it ... I couldn't, but it was no longer consuming my thoughts.

James and I had grown really close. He continued to assist me and pass down his tricks of the trade. I had officially been acclimated to the station and as his trusted companion.

One day, I answered the hotline, and it was a representative for *Mike Tyson*. He asked if I would allow *Mike Tyson* to come down to the station for an interview. Before I could answer, he added, ***"I'll throw in two tickets for the fight."*** *Iron Mike* was fighting *Andrew Golota* at the Palace in Auburn Hills.

Accepting trinkets and junkets was frowned upon in the news business, and I knew this.

So, I immediately told James, who was my supervisor, about the offer and informed him that two tickets were waiting for me in Pontiac.

Surprisingly, *James* agreed that it wouldn't cause any harm since the tickets were offered after I had agreed to the interview.

The young *Mike Tyson* came to the station for the interview. I wasn't there and didn't really care. I would see him at the fight. The tickets were valued at five hundred dollars. I figured they had to be ringside—so I thought.

During *Tyson's* visit to the station, he managed to insult one of the stagehands so badly that she sued him. He made a comment to the poor girl that even I was embarrassed when I heard what he said.

James gave me all the details. I thought, "What an asshole." I should've let one of the other stations have the interview. He seems to be a much better version of *Mike Tyson* now days. God bless him.

Then came fight night. I had grown up in the streets of Detroit, and my brother-in-law and sister were well-to-do and always attended the fights in Las Vegas, so I knew they would be at this fight. I was quite sure that all the Detroit hustlers and dealers from these streets would be at this fight.

We immediately looked for our seats. When we located them, we were blown away. Our $500 seats were in the nosebleed section. We were shocked. All this money for these seats—it was a rip-off. Luckily, we didn't pay for the tickets.

I shared a little bit of my past with James so that if we ran into any hustlers at the fight who knew me, it wouldn't be too uncomfortable for him. However, I was hoping I didn't see anyone from my old neighborhood. If I had, they might have wanted to reminisce about our street life or catch up on what I was doing these days.

So, I insisted we sit in our seats and wait for the fight. But *James* was enjoying the atmosphere and wanted to walk around until the fight started. After all, we had an hour or so before the main event. I hesitantly agreed and walked with him.

The first person we saw was *Chuck D* from Public Enemy. He remembered me from a Chicago hotel. He and *George Wallace* were there. *George* had stopped me in the lobby of the Holiday Inn and caused a scene by screaming, **"Where the hell have you been?"** I looked behind me because he was clearly talking to someone else. But he walked towards me and put his arm around me and continued to act as if we were old buddies. We had the attention of everyone in the lobby. I laughed so hard but then began playing along. He was great, and I'll never forget that! I love you, *George Wallace*.

James and I continued our journey inside the Palace of Auburn Hills. We then ran into *Chuck D* from Public Enemy. I chatted with him about the song lyrics and other writings of

mine that we had talked about while in Chicago. I gave him my business card and told him if he was still interested in my writing, I would be happy to share them. He never called.

I tried to head back to our seats at this point, but James wasn't having it. He wanted to walk some more. He was enjoying the social aspect of the huge crowd. We then saw Muhammad Ali's wife with her daughters, Laila, Maryum, and Rasheda. They were all so beautiful. I asked her if I could marry one of her daughters, and she laughed and said, **"Which one?"**

I responded, **"It doesn't matter. I just want to be in the family."**

We all laughed. If there had been a shaman, priest, or rabbi available, I would have married any of those women on the spot.

As we turned down another aisle, there stood my sister and brother-in-law. I thought, "Oh shit."

137

They were excited to see me and offered us two seats in their row. They had bought extra tickets that were much closer to the ring than ours. James was thrilled. I was hoping he didn't ask much about them as we stood there. He didn't but was excited about our new seats, which were much closer.

They gave us the tickets then pointed us in the direction of the seats then went in another direction. They, too, were enjoying socializing. James looked at me in amazement and said, ***"I'm glad we walked. Come on, let's go this way."***

I said, ***"No ... the fight's about to start in about ten minutes, and we're gonna have to make it to these seats and we don't even know where they are."***

He insisted, so we walked a bit more then make our way back to our seats, which were about ten rows from the ring. As we made our way to the seats, I saw *Timmy Jewel* from my old stomping grounds.

Timmy had left the drug game, opened a barbershop, and dabbled in the boxing promotion business. He was a small timer in this game, but he apparently had connections.

Timmy was excited to see me and insisted we sit with him. He had the best seats in the house and had two extra tickets, which were

ringside seats. We followed *Timmy*, ducked under the rope, and sat in our ringside seats. We were literally three rows from the ring.

There were four empty seats next to me.

I wondered who he had reserved those seats for. It didn't matter we were seated comfortably. *James* looked at me in disbelief.

The event was underway, and here we were, ringside. *Mike Tyson* had the Cash Money Boys (as they were known then) bring him out. *Lil*

Wayne, Birdman, Mannie Fresh, and *B.G.* opened the show, rapping and stomping around the ring.

Once they finished rapping and hyping the crowd up, they climbed out of the ring and headed toward us. The four empty seats next to me were theirs. We stood up and allowed them to get through to their seats. Each of them hugged me and gave me a dap as they walked by to take their seats.

James was in awe. He may have thought I knew them too. I just rolled with it. I had no idea this night would go like this, but it did. I was the talk at work the next day. *James* really gave me props. He was so cool. Basically, it was because of *James* that our good night turned out spectacular.

Years after my news days, I sometimes called James, who still works at the assignment desk at WDIV Detroit 4, and told him about good community stories taking place in Detroit. He always sent an available crew to cover the story. He was a good competitor, ally, and friend.

I covered a lot of good stories working there and had a lot of drama too. Presidential candidates always visited with their Secret Service. I remember when *George Bush Jr.* came to the station. The Secret Service swept the joint. First came the bomb-sniffing dogs, then the Secret Service agents themselves, before the candidate or president entered.

During *Bush's* visits, I chatted with one of his Secret Service agents at the assignment desk. She told me about their daily duties and then sold me on applying to become an agent. She took my information and said she would contact me.

A week later, I got a manila envelope in the mail. It was a packet from Quantico, Virginia. It contained paperwork to fill out and an invitation to the FBI headquarters.

I seriously considered joining. Then I read the paperwork and all the fine print. It said agents were forced to retire after a certain number of years on the beat. So, the senior agent from the movie In the Line of Fire with *Clint Eastwood* was a crock of shit. These bratty, know-it-all presidents are not putting their lives in the hands of some seventy-year-old agent who refuses to retire.

I never wanted to retire from anywhere. I wanted to work until the end. I never pursued the job. I had unfinished business in the news industry and was still excited about my duties there.

On September 11th, a normal news day took a tragic turn. Most of our monitors were tuned in to the national NBC News desk. When the first plane hit, everyone began watching the monitors and assumed it was some sort of fire at the World Trade Center.

We contacted the network, via the satellite booth, to send us a news feed of what they had on the fire. As we watched, we literally saw the second plane hit.

It went from zero to one hundred really fast around the newsroom. Before I knew it, everyone had come in. I listened as the news director shouting directives. He was putting people in place, and constant wire feeds from the AP and the network were coming nonstop. It was perfectly controlled chaos, and I took mental notes. I would have to draw upon them on October 7.

Once it had been confirmed as a terrorist attack, retaliation was imminent.

I usually worked weekends alone. And on Sunday, Operation Freedom shocked everyone. And now, it was my time to shine.

I was all alone at the assignment desk with a skeleton crew. When the war broke out, I immediately called every reporter I could. I had them meet photographers at specific locations. I had them at the Ambassador Bridge, at local mosques to get reactions, in Dearborn (the largest Middle Eastern community in the nation) for local reactions, and I had the chopper headed to the Blue Water Bridge in

Port Huron for any possible continued attacks at the borders. I even had reporters in downtown Detroit getting reactions from people.

Then I called the news director to advise him of what I had done.

He was at the station in 10 minutes.

When he came in, I informed him where I had positioned the team. I told him that I had called *James* as well but wanted to get everyone in place first. He was pleased. For once, there were people rushing into a crowded newsroom, and I already had teams in place. We were a like-minded group.

I never expected the war to break out so quickly, but we all anticipated it. I just happened to be alone at the control desk when it happened. This, to me, was my biggest achievement as a news guy. I was so proud of myself.

CHAPTER XXIX –
FALSE CLAIMS

Time passed. Things were back to normal in the newsroom, and I was still working at the assignment desk when *Bill Rice* called me about a homicide suspect being apprehended. I had no reporters available, so I went over to grab a quick soundbite from the chief.

When my photographer and I arrived, we entered the elevator and headed to the fourth floor. Two cops got on the elevator as well. As we ascended, I noticed the female cop glancing at me. She was attractive but didn't really stand out like *Scarlett Johansson* or *Beyoncé*. To break the awkward silence, I said, *"I've been a bad boy,"* then gestured with my hands in a surrendering pose and added,

"Arrest me."

The photographer laughed, and the male cop grinned, but the woman seemed unfazed, and her face remained stoic—as if she was a soldier at Windsor Castle in London trying not to break character.

We got off the elevator, and the interview went smoothly. Ten minutes after we arrived back at the station, I answered a call at the assignment desk while the photographer edited the tape for the news show.

The voice on the phone asked for me directly. I said, *"Speaking."*

He began ranting:

"You son of a bitch, if you ever come over here harassing my officers again, I'll come over there and arrest your ass!"

I thought it was a prank, so I hung up on the caller. He immediately called back and picked up where he'd left off. ***"Oh, you think this is a joke?"***

So, I asked who it was, and he replied, ***"Captain Davis!"*** He began threatening to come and arrest me again. I seriously wondered if *Uncle Tomboy* had put him up to this.

I told him I didn't know what this was about but that there was, apparently, some sort of mix-up. He described the two officers in the elevator and claimed they had reported me to him in a complaint. This had just gotten serious. I asked him, ***"If the cops felt threatened, why hadn't they arrested me on the elevator?"*** He then accused me

of being a smart ass and, again, threatened to come and arrest me. By now, I'd had enough of these threats.

I told him not to call me back. If he wanted to arrest me, then come to the station and do it. Otherwise, call and talk to my news director. Then I hung up on him. I immediately went to inform my news director of what had just happened.

Sure enough, the officer called back as I returned to my desk. I had them transfer the call into my news director's office as requested.

Five minutes later, I was summoned into his office with two producers, an assistant, and even the general manager was present.

As I sat, they questioned me about the incident and asked me to explain exactly what happened on the elevator. I explained everything and advised them that the photographer could vouch for me. We had never left each other's presence the entire time I was there. They called him in, and he verified everything I said.

Everyone looked puzzled wondering why this officer would call over with such nasty accusations against me. As we sat there, I kept trying to visualize the female cop (who looked familiar). But my team had made up their minds.

The general manager said, *"Fuck him! And if he calls back, have him call me."* My fears turned to excitement.

But I still wondered why the female officer looked familiar to me.

I never attended any of my high school reunions. But my buddy Kevin implored me to attend Cody's reunion with him in 2017. He had been in touch with some of the guys and girls over the past fifteen to twenty years, and they'd asked about me and wanted to see me.

I decided attend the reunion and chat with my high school friends about old times. The reunion was held on the Cody High School campus, but a few of us, the junior and varsity basketball players— planned a barbecue at Belle Isle the next day. I was happy to see the guys and see how well they were doing for themselves. It was great.

When we got to Belle Isle, the old basketball team members showed up, but a couple of girls came as well.

One of the girls seemed to take an interest in me. She even made me a hot dog with all the fixings and brought it over to me. So, I asked

my friend *Carleton* who she was. He seemed surprised that I didn't remember her.

He said, *"You don't remember her?"* Then continued, *"That's Lisa. She lived a couple of houses down from me."*

He lived three blocks over, and I never really visited him when we were younger, so I didn't personally know the girl. But she did look familiar. Then it hit me. When I was in high school, my buddy and I planned to skip school and meet two girls at the railroad tracks. We were going to have some fun at his house. When we got to the tracks where the girls were, I changed my mind and went back to school. The girls got upset.

My buddy later told me that the girl I was supposed to hook up with, thought I wasn't attracted to her, so she had an attitude. I didn't care—I wasn't interested at the time.

Before we left the park during our extended high school reunion, the girl that made my hot dog asked for my number. I was pleased, and we exchanged numbers. To my surprise, she called me about an hour later.

We talked and made plans to meet up later that night for a dinner date. I was surprised that she never asked me what I did for a living and never said what she did.

So, I took the initiative and asked what she did. She told me she was a cop. My stomach dropped. It all came back. Just then, I remembered her from that elevator years earlier, as well as the railroad incident back in high school. I asked her what precinct she worked out of, to be certain. She confirmed she worked out of the downtown precinct in Detroit.

I immediately made an excuse and canceled the dinner date. I never called her again.

The last thing I needed was a psycho cop in my life.

CHAPTER XXX –
ENTERING A NEW FIELD

I began contemplating if I wanted another career path. I wasn't having the **life impact** I wanted in the news industry. I did not want to let my supporters down, but I wanted to make a larger impact in life and on people in general. I guess I got bored and needed a change.

I had always wanted to write books and plays. I wrote material but rarely let others read them. I had multiple drafts of incomplete books and even published a couple on Amazon under a pseudonym, only to pull them later. They were not the material I really wanted to write about. To me, they weren't good enough. Besides, I was my own worst critic and thought nothing was ever good enough. All my writings became ongoing, ever-changing, incomplete works of fiction or fantasy.

Martha, a retired schoolteacher, had implored me for years to teach. After all, she had become my best friend over the years, and I had confided so much in her that she knew me well. She knew me better than anyone else in this world. She thought I was destined to teach and knew how much I loved kids. She also knew about my unfulfilled urge to make a significant difference in life.

I didn't exactly lose interest in the news business. I simply did not feel the same about Channel 4 as I had about WXYZ or WJRT. I felt at home while working for the previous stations. I wondered if I'd become burnt out in the industry. Nevertheless, the interest just wasn't there anymore. I never wanted to do print or radio, but I really considered both at this point. I later got the chance to do radio with a buddy, but it was short-lived.

I left the news industry and began teaching at George Washington Carver Academy. I taught all subjects and applied for, and received, a temporary teaching certificate every year while taking a class or two at the local college.

This was a charter school, and I began teaching 4th grade. It was a predominantly black district. Deputy Director *Robert (Bob) Austin* was in total charge and let it be known. He came from Louisiana to represent one of the biggest restaurateurs in the city of Detroit and

wound up running the school. As deputy director, he oversaw everything at the school.

I was extremely enthusiastic about teaching. I absolutely loved it. The pay wasn't great, but it didn't matter because I loved what I was doing. I even taught kindergarten in summer school during our breaks. Those babies were the cutest creatures I had ever seen. They cried when they could not get their way but they loved me. And when I nurtured them, they were willing to learn everything I taught them.

It's amazing what lengths kids will go to for you when you show them that you genuinely love them. I loved those kids more than life itself. And they knew it.

If I had lived a traditional life, I would have had as many kids as my wife would have allowed. There is no greater joy in this life than seeing happy children.

Bob and Principal *Marci Wade* called me into the office and explained that I would be required to connect with the larger and more troubled kids. They were convinced that I could manage them much better than the other teachers. So, they handpicked my students.

True to form, they made sure all the challenging kids were in my class. I was up for the task, though. I had finally done it. *Martha* had insisted I was cut out for this, and here I was—teaching.

147

The first week, we socialized. I got to know them, they got to know me, and they got to know each other. I established a social connection among my kids early. I wanted to make sure they loved one another as I loved them. I had them assist each other and began grading them in groups.

The next step was the real challenge, and it had to be resolved fast. The State of Michigan had the Grade Level Content Expectations (GLCE) in place—we called them the Gli-kees. There was a lot of pressure to get the students up to par with their grade learning levels.

I began to work hard with them on their independence, where a lot of them struggled. I had my work cut out for me. But they were great kids and were trying their hardest. During a parent-teacher conference, I hatched a plan. I wanted the parents' permission to take the kids to the main library in Midtown Detroit on Saturdays. But I needed the parents to drop them off. I assured them that if the students showed

up and studied for an hour, I would buy them pizza for lunch. We even went to the Butterfly when I could get them there. My girlfriend (at the time) was willing to help me keep an eye on them. There, they played arcade games and ate pizza.

You can imagine how I struggled doing this on a teacher's salary. But I managed to get it done. Once or twice, a parent would offer a donation of twenty dollars. I was appreciative.

Three kids consistently showed up. One of them had no academic issues. She passed every test I ever gave her with an A grade, but I wasn't going to turn her away. She became my trusted volunteer and helped me keep the other students focused. They wanted to be like her. And if I could lift their grades, it would increase the overall percentage of the class.

The other two students' grades jumped during the weekly tests. And when they talked about the pizza and games to the other students in our classroom, they wanted in. My numbers grew. More of my struggling students were now showing up.

Some of the parents were taking advantage of the situation, though. Before I knew it, they were dropping off two or three of their kids, claiming they wanted to stay with their brothers or sisters. Now I was running a latchkey facility. It was embarrassing, but it didn't deter me. These were my kids now. And my efforts would pay off. I just knew it.

The Saturday tutoring sessions worked. My students continued to study hard for me.

They even requested that we meet on Sundays as well. On my salary, I just couldn't. I was overjoyed that they were willing to extend our study times, but I simply could not meet them on Sundays. It turned out, extra tutoring sessions were not needed. Twenty-three out of thirty-three students enrolled in my class made the honor roll at the end of the year. I was ecstatic. I did not have a failing student in my entire class.

The principal thought it would be best if I taught fifth grade the following year since most of my students' parents wanted me with their kids. I personally thought they needed a different learning perspective from another teacher, but I was honored. So, I

agreed, and the principal moved me up a grade level and assigned as many of the same kids to my class as she could.

I never really had to discipline any of the kids. And when I did, it hurt me more than it hurt them. I can recall one incident in which a student refused to finish her work.

She made excuses after excuses to get out of completing her daily assignments. I wanted her to at least try so that I could gauge her learning levels. She was a new student and simply wanted to be my favorite but never wanted to complete her work.

Once, she didn't write anything on her essay assignment, so I kept her from recess.

When I got back to the classroom with the students, my assistant informed me the girl had gone to the office. I was later summoned to the office by the principal and the deputy director. I sensed trouble because they requested a social worker's presence as well.

I asked what this was all about, and they informed me that the student had levied some serious allegations against me. My heart was racing. I braced myself for the lie. They then proceeded to inform me that the student claimed she saw marijuana in my drawer and that I was smoking it with some of the other kids during recess.

I was relieved. My heartbeat slowed to a normal pace again. At their request, I followed them back to my classroom and let them search my desk. They interviewed a few students and then realized the accusations were baseless. I assumed it was a formality and that they knew better. But they had their procedures and were following protocol.

I immediately requested that the student be transferred out of my classroom or I would quit. It pained me more than you'll ever know, but I had to get her out of my classroom. I really wanted to help her, but had her lie been of a different nature, I could still be dealing with the repercussions of it to this day. I was not going to allow her a second chance to levy another lie against me.

During the final semester, my fifth-grade students threw me a surprise end-of-the-year party. All of my students were in on it and swore my principal and deputy director to secrecy. I didn't have a clue.

These fifth graders must have spent five hundred dollars on cakes, decorations, gifts, and school supplies. I fell in love with each and every one of them all over again. I was trying to speak but I could barely get the words out, because I cried like a baby in front of my class and those in attendance. The tears weren't just for the party, but because I would not have the same group next year. They were moving on.

The following semester, I would have a whole new bunch. These students impacted me way more than I impacted them.

The deputy director and the principal were so impressed with the effect I had on the students that they asked me to join a contest in a black-owned Chicago newspaper. The subject was, *Your approach towards education and how it impacted you?* The winner would get five hundred dollars and a published article.

I entered with a story in which I expressed the passion and commitment it takes to teach and what it took to be a great teacher. I also shared my communication and delivery approach to teaching techniques.

I never expected to win, but I knew the article was very well-written. A week later, I was provided ten copies of the newspaper containing the article. I won. There was my article—PUBLISHED. I never saw a dime of the money, though. Since the principal and deputy director entered me in the contest, I assumed they took what they thought they were entitled to. But it was certainly without my consent. Unfortunately, my copies were damaged in my flooded basement.

CHAPTER XXXI – THE SCUMBAG

Things got interesting. I was later assigned as a writing coach and as Assistant MEAP Coordinator for the school. I also attracted unwanted special attention from *Bob* and *Marci*.

I was summoned to the office by *Bob* about two to three times a week. He always sent a substitute teacher to my classroom to cover the afternoon courses.

I had no idea what this was about, but I found myself at Floods Bar & Grill in downtown Detroit in the early afternoons. He insisted we take his shiny new Corvette. He thought the car impressed me, but I hated that car. It was one of the most uncomfortable rides I had ever taken. It was so small that I had trouble getting out of it. The car sat so low that I felt every bump and was always paranoid about being in an accident. It was apparent that safety was not its best feature.

We would meet up with his buddies. It was always the same group of gentlemen. There was *Steven Hood*, the brother of *Nicholas*, who'd lost his bid for mayor of Detroit every time he ran, yet this group introduced him as one of the *Hood* family dynasty members. Then there was *Judge Strong*, the flamboyant municipal court judge who, to this day, always asks about *Bob* when I see him—and lastly, there was *Killer Kilpatrick*—dad of the infamous Detroit mayor, *Kwame Kilpatrick*.

I was impressed by *Bob's* Harvard Law degree. I was even impressed with some of the company he kept. But I hated it when he went out of his way to try and impress me. He would introduce me to Detroit landmarks like the Detroit Institute of Arts (DIA) and Sinbad's Restaurant as places I needed to experience. He had no idea that I frequented those places numerous times. I was Detroit, and he didn't have a clue. He always introduced me as if I were a sheltered young man and thought that he was broadening my horizons.

However, we drank merrily and had fun times at Floods. But every time I left my kids to join this group of guys, I felt a sense of regret. I hated leaving my students.

I did not start teaching so that I could abandon my kids. This wasn't a part of the job for me. And yes, I was grateful they hired me,

but my passion and commitment to the students was real. I loved being with them.

These class interruptions to visit Floods were wearing on me. I was losing respect for *Bob*.

I finally asked if he would not take me from my students and advised that I would be available after classes to join him and his team at Floods. He wasn't hearing it and wanted to flex his authority to continue to impress me. Classroom interferences to visit Floods seemed to be coming a part of my curriculum, and I was becoming more and more unimpressed with this guy. I began to loathe him.

Refusing some of the invitations caused an obvious rift in our relationship. I knew it would probably cost me my job eventually, but I loved teaching, and that was more important to me than hanging out with these guys. Teaching didn't pay much, but the real reward was what my passion and commitment yielded. The students were becoming smarter and better young adults because of me.

Eventually, *Bob* appeared to get the message. Because a week after our last Floods visit, he and *Principal Wade* asked me to hang out after work. They, again, wanted to impress me with the company they kept. They bragged that the bar we were visiting was owned by a special friend who served as a medical doctor by day. They described him as a real mover and shaker in the city. He owned the bar on West 7 Mile Road just west of Greenfield Road.

He was none other than *Doctor Buoyae*. They introduced me as "the rookie" who they wanted to introduce to important people in Detroit ... They were sort of showing me the ropes. I played as if I was impressed again. They had no idea how long *Doctor Buoyae* and I had known each other or how long he had been involved with my family and I wasn't going to tell them. He played ignorantly of it as well. He then whispered to me to come back and enjoy myself without them.

Fifteen years later, my niece still worked at *Doctor Buoyae's* private practice as his nurse. Back when they were trying to impress me, she was his nurse's assistant. *Doctor Buoyae* also pastored my mother's funeral just a few years ago.

I was at the school two years before *Bob* and *Marci* took over as principal and deputy director. Prior to their arrival, *Felisha* and I had

taught together at the school. She was a very attractive Italian/Black woman. We'd gotten to know one another and would go out to lunch and dinner after work about twice a week.

She was seeking her master's degree in education and occasionally helped me with my lesson plans. She had two beautiful kids. I fell in love with her kids the moment I met them as well.

Felisha was so smart that she decided to continue going to school while we taught. She begged me to enroll so that we could earn advanced degrees together. She had been accustomed to taking fifteen to twenty credit hours a semester, working more than fifty hours a week as a teacher, and maintaining a 4.0 with ease. I could not keep up with this woman. She was on a whole other level.

She always asked me to come over to her house, and I never hesitated. I often fell asleep on her bed while she stayed up late studying. The next day, we would head out to work. I wanted to date her so badly, but I wanted her to make the first move. I liked her and didn't want to mess things up by acting on a lustful urge.

If I was going to get married, I had hoped it would be to her. She was beautiful, smart, and raising wonderful little girls alone. But she shot that notion of us dating down quickly. She said she liked me but didn't want to cross the line and damage our friendship. And I respected that. So, we continued our relationship just the way it was for three years.

One night, she laid on the bed with me and started toying with my ears to wake me up. I think she understood that I was never going to make the first move, so she began to initiate something. I wanted her to be totally comfortable with anything that happened between us. But tonight, I was tired, and she was irritating me, so I got up and moved to the couch to sleep.

When I fell asleep on the couch, she came there and started rubbing a straw against my ear, so I grabbed her in a bear hug. As I looked in her eyes, her smile turned serious. She asked me to come back to the bedroom.

I had a look of confusion. She had a look of passion. I really didn't want to damage our friendship, but I followed her to the bedroom anyway.

I lay down on the bed, and she said she didn't want me wearing my clothes on her sheets and pulled back the blankets. I undressed and lay in bed. She lay next to me. To my surprise, she wiggled herself under me, so I kissed her. The next thing I remember is taking off her pajama bottoms and removing my shorts. We were looking into each other's eyes and making love. It was an unbelievable dream come true for me.

We both knew this was long overdue. I knew she had tons of admirers, and she may have been a little out of my league, but I wanted her. I had to have her as my girlfriend, then my wife. This was the one.

But then she abruptly stopped me after five minutes. I thought I had done something wrong. She expressed that we had moved too fast. I was disappointed. I should have resisted before I acted on my impulses, I thought. Now, I may have fucked things up forever.

155

As time went on, we, surprisingly, remained the closest of friends. I completely trusted her, and she trusted me again. We took trips to Cedar Point with the kids. It was weird to be so close after our failed intimacy attempt. I had never experienced this type of friendship with a woman before, but it was great. She was still as desirable as I had ever seen her, but now, I saw her differently. I began seeing her as a true friend.

I began dating other women as she had suggested. She dated other men as well. She shared intimate details about the men she dated. I pretty much gave up on any kind of serious, intimate relationship with her after that and I think she sensed it too.

So, months later, I was shocked when, unexpectedly, she offered me a specific ultimatum. She insisted I make a pinky promise right then and there. The promise was that in five years, if we weren't married to other people, we would marry each other.

Ironically, this promise gave me a deep, intense feeling of satisfaction and confusion. I liked this woman. So, I agreed. I had concerns and thought we simply moved too fast the first time. Now, we had become even closer friends and hadn't given in to any further intimate urges. So, I thought maybe this time it could work.

I believed that if we got married, it would be a marriage based on trust and familiarity.

We weren't going to be the couple that never really got to know one another until well into a marriage—when it may have been too late.

She got her master's and was now pursuing her Ph.D. She had taken an assistant principal's position on the east side of Detroit. She still called me faithfully and occasionally came to my school to take me to lunch.

We helped each other prep for MEAP testing. She continuously helped with my weekly lesson plans. She begged me to come teach at her school, but at this point, I was way too committed to my kids. I couldn't do it.

The woman never stopped going to school and, surprisingly, still maintained a 4.0 all the way through.

She was determined and wanted me right beside her. But I couldn't commit to school like that while working so many hours. I wanted my master's though, and Marygrove College was where I applied. They had a Griot program that offered an accelerated master's degree along with a business degree. I applied and got in. *Felisha* was so happy for me. Turns out, the accelerated courses were too much for me while I worked full time. *Felisha* was upset when I dropped out.

Her ability to constantly pursue higher education and do it while working full time was nothing short of miraculous. And to maintain a

4.0 doing it for all those years was beyond me. Before I knew it, she had her Ph.D. in Early Childhood Education. And now, she insisted, with a sly smirk, that I call her doctor *Felisha*. I was so proud of her. She was now *Doctor Fee Fee* to me.

She dropped by George Washington Carver Academy, where I worked, to take me out to lunch one day. We were going to celebrate her newfound title. We went to Fishbones and enjoyed some Creole food. Then it was back to the grind.

When she dropped me off, *Bob* summoned me to his office. He wasn't summoning me to take me out or impress me with the company he kept. This time, he wanted to know who the woman was that I went to lunch with.

I assumed he'd known her or maybe seen her somewhere before. But he simply saw her drop me off at the school from our lunch date

and thought she was beautiful. He wanted to meet her. He wanted me to play matchmaker between the two. He insisted I tell her his net worth. According to him, he was worth two to three million dollars. I assumed he was, but I knew that telling *Felisha* would have ruined his chances with her. She hated arrogance. So, I told him I would make the introduction, but I would let him mention his own accomplishments.

I had known *Felisha* for years. I thought he'd be the last person she wanted to go on a date with. He was short, older, wealthy, and extremely braggadocious. I assumed she would shoot him down immediately.

Felisha was willing to meet him but wanted me to accompany them on the date. She suggested Union Street. I knew the place well from my poetry reading days.

On the date of the meeting, we were running twenty minutes behind, so I called her to let her know. She didn't mind. She was running a little late as well.

Then *Bob* wanted to make another stop, and I knew it would put us even further behind.

He was not respecting her time. I advised her that we were running more behind so that she would not be sitting there alone for nearly an hour. She let out a disappointed sigh and said she wouldn't wait there all night.

When we arrived, she was nowhere to be found, so I called her. When she picked up, she said she got tired of waiting, then advised me that she would try to come back. I knew that it was unlikely that she would make it back.

I wasn't upset. I remembered our pinky agreement, anyway.

As we finished our first round of drinks, I got up to use the men's room. When I got back, *Bob* was sitting and laughing at the bar with two very beautiful women, so I joined them.

We chatted with them for an hour or so while we waited on *Felisha*. By this time, I knew she wasn't coming back. She stopped answering her phone, so I assumed she went to bed. So, I made the best of my night.

I sat next to *Tanya* ... one of the nicest and most beautiful women I had ever seen. And we struck up a conversation that went well. I remember us laughing and making a wager about who was older.

She won the bet and laughed, then shared her chicken wings with me. It was obvious that this chance meeting was going somewhere.

But suddenly, *Bob* began to rush me out of the bar. *Tanya* wanted me to stay. The *Erykah Badu* concert they were attending didn't start for another hour or so.

Bob had no more patience and insisted I leave with him now or catch a cab back to the school where my car was. I asked him why he wanted to leave so abruptly, and he said he was tired. I didn't believe that, but we left. *Tanya* called me after the concert. And we were inseparable from that night on.

A few days later, I talked to the woman, *Belinda*, who *Bob* sat next to at the bar, and asked her if she ever got to know him after that night. She said he bragged about his Harvard Law degree all night. She admitted that the law degree was impressive but added, ***"Maybe that clown should have attended Howard University instead,"*** then continued, ***"He would have been more cultured, and his approach may have been more respectful."***

Belinda's resume was impressive. She had a master's degree herself and had worked for the United States Department of Defense for years before retiring. She was classy, owned a beautiful home, was always well-dressed, and she was single. *Bob's* resume was extremely impressive, but you threw in their personalities, and Belinda was way out of his league.

CHAPTER XXXII –
HER TRUE INTENTIONS

I couldn't wait to tell *Felisha* about *Tanya*. It had only been two years since she issued the five-year ultimatum. There were still three years left, so I had not violated the terms of our agreement.

Besides, I knew *Felisha* well enough to know she'd be over the moon for me about my new girlfriend.

She was dating as well. I was almost certain she was still seeing one of the guys she had introduced me to. Most of her suitors were short-lived and did not work out.

Nonetheless, she was dating, so I knew she'd be happy for me.

Tanya and I grew into something special, amazingly fast. I was stoked. She had nothing to hide and always answered her phone for me when I called her and even answered it in front of me when I was with her. This eliminated a lot of the guesswork and suspicion about who she was. I had not felt this confident in a relationship since my college days.

Sure enough, when I broke the news to *Felisha*, she was happy for me, and that's why I loved her. I had always told *Tanya* all about *Felisha* and vice versa.

Tanya and I visited each other every day. When her lease was up, we decided to get a condo together. Of course, I talked to *Felisha* about it prior to pulling the trigger. I invited her and the girls over when we got situated in our new place. She and *Tanya* became close friends. I never kept anything about *Felisha* from *Tanya* ... even the fact that we'd once slept together.

Occasionally, I would come home from work, and the two of them would be there chatting and laughing at the dining room table. We ate dinner together, and *Felisha* occasionally accompanied us to the movies. These were my two best friends. I felt complete.

Bob and *Marci* hated the fact that I was no longer available to hang out with them. I actually missed *Judge Strong*. He was extremely entertaining. He was a bit flamboyant but very entertaining.

I introduced *Marci* and *Bob* to *Tanya*. We were inseparable, and they knew it. I knew my days were numbered at school because I no longer had time for them outside of work.

Sure enough, they didn't renewed my contract the following semester.

Felisha began to understand just how serious my relationship was with *Tanya*, then things suddenly changed. On one occasion, the phone rang at 12:30 a.m. *Tanya* and I were both awakened from our sleep. It was *Felisha* calling from Beaumont Hospital in Royal Oak.

She'd been rushed there for an infection. I had to go. She told me that her cat had bitten her on the hand, and it had gotten infected. She needed a ride home. Tanya insisted we go together. I thought, no big deal.

We arrived at the hospital, but she wasn't there. She had begun walking down Thirteen Mile Road at 1 a.m., hoping to see my car making the turn onto Thirteen Mile. *Tanya* was extremely alarmed and warned her that she could have been raped walking all alone at this time of night.

She laughed and responded, ***"I'm so horny, that a sexual encounter at this point would've probably been welcomed."***

Tanya looked at me as if she'd read my mind. I listened to their small talk and never said another word enroute to Felisha's house. *Tanya*

161

was glad she decided to ride with me that night.

On another occasion, *Felisha* asked me to see if *Tanya* would have a problem if she took me out to dinner on my birthday? *Tanya* insisted that lunch would be more appropriate. I immediately thought about the Beaumont incident and agreed with *Tanya's* decision.

Lunch it was. It was understood that I had to be at the Renaissance Center to pick *Tanya* up from work at 4 p.m. sharp. *Felisha* agreed but insisted she drive since it was my birthday. We did Mongolian Barbecue in Royal Oak. It was great. I kept track of time so that I wouldn't be late picking *Tanya* up from work. She was so punctual and I didn't want to give her any reason not to trust my friendship with *Felisha*.

We left Mongolian Barbecue in plenty of time for me to make it back to my house, get the car, and pick up *Tanya*. But then suddenly,

Felisha wanted to make a quick stop at a friend's house. We were now cutting it close, and I began to worry about the time. After we left her friend's house, she pulled into a bank drive-through line, and cars pulled in behind us ... trapping us.

At this point, I was a little perturbed by her actions and called *Tanya* immediately to explain why I was going to be late. She was not happy. She was so punctual, and I knew how she felt.

Felisha yelled in the background, ***"He's going to make it."*** I knew I wasn't going to make it on time. *Felisha* was purposefully wasting time. I was thirty minutes late picking *Tanya* up.

Tanya let me know that my friendship with *Felisha* was suddenly taking a toll on our relationship. I understood. Even after issuing the warning, she remained happy and continued to be the fun-loving person she'd always been since I met her. I often looked at her and imagined losing her over my friendship with *Felisha*. I could not bear the thought of it. So, I scaled my time with *Felisha*, drastically and

162

proposed to *Tanya.*

She and I had been living together for a year. I learned to put the toilet seat down; we showered together occasionally. It was time. I took her to the jeweler and asked her which ring she liked. She was extremely pleased and picked out a beautiful one. I was now getting married, who knew?

I wanted to break the engagement news to *Felisha.* So, I offered to take her to lunch.

Tanya was visiting her mom and chose not to join us but gave me permission to go. I promised her that I was going to break the engagement news to *Felisha,* and she warned me to be careful.

When I told her that *Tanya* and I were getting married, she seemed genuinely happy for us but questioned me about how well I really knew *Tanya.* I assured her that I was very comfortable with my decision.

I joked about our pinky promise and said, ***"Two more years, and it would have been you and me."*** She gave me a look of disgust and continued to eat. I was floored by her reaction.

The marriage was great. *Tanya* never wanted kids, and I accepted that. However, I thought that was selfish on her behalf because I knew

she would be a great mom. But I only wanted to satisfy her, and I was happy as a clam.

The next time I saw *Felisha* was at a teachers' conference at Cobo Arena. There were close to ten thousand teachers there. How she singled me out, I will never know. She confronted me and caused a scene, yelling, ***"We were best friends, and we were supposed to be married. You meet a woman and end our friendship, just like that!"***

163

I grabbed her and pulled her into a storage closet and pleaded with her to calm down. I assured her that we were still friends and that I just didn't want to make *Tanya* uncomfortable. She assured me that I married the wrong woman.

I left the event early. It would be years before I talked to *Felisha* again. When I did, I learned that she had become a grandma and was loving it. She seemed so content, and I was happy for her.

CHAPTER XXXIII –
FINDING MYSELF AGAIN

*M*arci and *Bob* never called me back the following semester. Halfway through the school year, they were ousted due to their clandestine actions regarding school fundings and a new principal was in charge.

My wife, *Tanya* hated me working for them anyway, but I missed being in those kids' lives.

Years later, I ran into a few of my students downtown. My little cousin *Durrell Summers* played basketball for Michigan State University (MSU), and the team made it to the Final Four. The tournament was played at Ford Field in Detroit. I was there to watch them work out and saw my old students.

The students were as excited as I was to reunite. They hugged me, and each one of them had a story to tell of our times together. We forgot about the Spartans for about thirty minutes. I spent two years with these kids as my students. It was so touching to see them again. Apparently, they had formed a bond outside the classroom and still hung out with each other all these years later.

I picked up odd jobs just to support myself and my marriage. I worked at OnStar for about two years. It was great. I got really good at it—so much so that they moved me upstairs and had me monitoring calls. I rarely followed the script but knew how to talk to people and provide accurate directions. Hell, I had given directions to photographers and reporters for years. I was great at it. I guess they plucked the right guy from the advisor's floor.

The most memorable call I got was from *Joe Piscopo* of Saturday Night Live. *Eddie Murphy* and *Jim Belushi* were my favorite SNL characters. But I'll never forget the skit where *Eddie* played *Stevie Wonder*, and *Piscopo* played *Frank Sinatra*.

That skit was so funny to me that I still laugh just thinking about it. So, when *Joe* called and I saw the last name, I did a double take.

I asked if he was **the** *Joe Piscopo* from Saturday Night Live and he assured me he was. I assumed by the voice and the humor that it was *Joe* from Saturday Night Live.

I told him that he was half of the duo from my favorite SNL skit. I explained which skit it was. He told me he enjoyed the skit as well. After he laughed and joked with me, he commented on his kids. He had so many kids, but he was happy and proud that he had them. He said it was rough being responsible for so many kids. I told him that I understood and that he was a stand-up guy for caring so much for them. However, I begged him to perform the "Ebony and Ivory" skit for me right then and there—and he did.

I was taken aback when he started. I interrupted him and asked him to stop and start over while I put him on speaker. To my surprise, he did. There must have been thirty advisors surrounding my desk singing along to *Joe Piscopo* performing his rendition of "Ebony and Ivory" as *Frank Sinatra*.

After that personal performance, he cracked my top six list as one of my all-time favorites from SNL: *Eddie Murphy, Jim Belushi, Phil Hartman, Gilda Radner, and Tim Meadows* rounded out my top six.

I then began working for a nonprofit organization in the Detroit Public Schools. My job was to establish resource centers in chosen schools and assist parents in understanding Title One funding. I educated them about their roles and responsibilities in spending those funds.

The state allocated the funds to the schools, and parents had no idea of their rights to a portion of those funds. I really enjoyed helping the parents become more invested in their kids' lives.

Parents were entitled to use a room at their kids' schools. They could also use Title I funds (1% of the total Title I funding allocated to that school) to stock those rooms with computers, paper, pens, and anything educationally related as long as the budget contained enough funds. The students were allowed to use the room during breaks and after class as well.

I was the project manager who took over for my buddy, *Lee Fitzpatrick*. I worked under his tutelage for a couple of years prior to taking the reins. *Lee* decided to take an assistant principal job in the Alpena school district. He insisted I take over his position as project manager.

Lee was a six-foot-eight white guy who was not only my supervisor but my best friend on the job.

He had worked in this predominantly Black school district and was loved by all the students.

The kids flocked to him every time he showed up at their school. They may have thought he was once a pro ball player because of his height. Nevertheless, they loved him. Although I appreciated his campaigning for me to take his position, I hated seeing him leave.

I had more than thirty schools located on the eastside of Detroit to visit weekly. Lee made it look so easy, but it was taxing. The true joy I got out of it was educating the parents about their rights and helping the students in the resource centers.

Marcus Garvey Academy was where my office was. The principal had no issues with what we were doing. *Principal Hearns* and his staff at Marcus Garvey Academy were very generous. They often brought me lunch during their school events. And I helped them out when I could.

Target was awarding funds to a few schools around the state of Michigan to upgrade their libraries. They offered a one-hundred-thousand-dollar stipend as part of their Education Initiative push.

They visited quite a few schools before they made their decision and we were one of the schools on their list. The principal asked me to speak at the event, but he had only given me about an hour's prior notice, leaving me little time to prepare. I was nervous but knew they needed the money, so I agreed to speak. The principal began his speech before the round table of Target executives. I expected one of his staff members to speak next, but he gestured to me and introduced me as a parent liaison for the school.

I gave the school kudos for their assistance and continued to speak on behalf of the parents. I mentioned that if granted these funds, the principal was willing to allow parents not only access to the resource center but also access to the newly renovated library.

I also explained that with these added resources, parents could further assist in the educational process and monitor their own kids while eliminating a lot of the pressure on the teachers.

I knew the principal had not agreed to this, but he put me on the spot and hadn't given me time to rehearse, so I put him on the spot and obligated him to this commitment (if awarded the funds).

Turns out, it worked. As soon as I finished speaking, the Target members applauded and awarded Marcus Garvey Academy a one-hundred-thousand-dollar check.

I never mentioned my audible (a sudden change of a play used in football games) to the principal, and he never mentioned the fact that I had put him on the hook to allow the parents access to the new and improved library.

I altered the play, scored a victory for the parents, and felt great about it.

CHAPTER XXXIV – A SHOCKING DIAGNOSIS

For the first time in my life, I found myself working two jobs. Here I was with two degrees and years of experience yet working two mediocre jobs to make ends meet.

But *Tanya* and I wanted to buy a house together. The economy had taken a turn for the worse, but the good thing was that it was a buyer's market. My full-time job at a call center and my part-time job at Home Depot would help us achieve our goal. I was excited about the Home Depot job; it allowed me to buy all the tools I wanted at a discount.

I convinced *Tanya* that we should buy a bank-owned home so that we didn't have to spend a lot of money on it and could fix it up. I also advised her that we could make a profit if and when we sold it.

She would have preferred to spend less on a small bungalow. I, on the other hand, figured if we were going to spend over one hundred thousand dollars on a home in 2008, it made more sense to spend it on a bank-owned home and fix it up.

I found one in Farmington Hills, and she really liked it, but there was too much work needed in the house. She was concerned that I would not be able to complete the work on the house and that we would have to pay a contractor. I knew I had some skills and figured it couldn't be that hard.

Although she doubted my skills, we bought the house. She challenged me, but I reassured her that I could do the work. *"My father worked construction,"* I assured her, *"and I picked up a lot of his skills."*

I didn't tell her my dad was a cement mason, not a carpenter, but he did a lot of carpentry and everything else and around our house.

I picked the perfect house, surrounded by trees in a great neighborhood. She agreed, so we bought it, and the timing couldn't have been better. In 2008, the market was down, so we got a great deal.

I worked on that house for a whole year. I found and purchased marble to match what was half done in the home and completed it. I installed window wells and windows in the empty spaces and I painted the entire house.

She was flabbergasted and bragged to her friends about the repairs.

To tell you the truth, I was just as amazed as she was. I had no idea I had these skills.

Nevertheless, I have to give a lot of credit where credit is due: Thank you, Dad, and thank you, YouTube.

Farmington Hills was great. *Tanya* and I now owned a house with plenty of privacy and property. We weren't stacked on top of our neighbors, and I needed the space. I was initially reluctant to move there. I had heard stories about the Farmington Hills police prior to moving there, which, luckily, turned out to be false.

Years earlier, my buddies told me that the Farmington Hills police hated Black people.

That was certainly not true, at least for Black Farmington Hills residents.

I'd been stopped for speeding on a couple of occasions but was let off the hook with a warning.

In one incident, the Farmington Hills cop stopped me for doing sixty mph in a forty-five-mph zone. I had forgotten I left my loaded pistol on the front passenger seat because the holster was hurting my hip.

When the officer approached the passenger-side door, she asked me why I traveled with a pistol on my seat. I was so shocked that it was there, that I inadvertently reached for it to put it away.

She screamed, *"No!"* I froze in my tracks. She politely took the gun and put it on the passenger floor area. She then asked for my driver's license. I handed it to her along with my CPL license and proof of insurance then she walked to her vehicle. Two minutes later, she came back to the vehicle, handed it all back, and asked me to be careful.

She had every right to blow me away for reaching for that gun but chose not to. I was extremely lucky that night because I knew just what

the headlines would have read the next day: White Cop Kills Black Man for Speeding. Poor woman would have been stigmatized for the rest of her life.

I was so comfortable in Farmington Hills that I asked my mom to come live with us. She laughed it off. She wasn't leaving Detroit. I could have had a mansion with servants in West Bloomfield, and she still wouldn't have left Detroit to come live with me.

Other than teaching in Detroit, I hadn't lived there for quite a while. But I managed to get back every other day. I played weekly poker with the guys and occasionally sat and chatted with my mom. She was older, and I always loved sitting with her.

My mother was now eighty-two years old and managed to tell me, quite often, how proud she was of me. I was proud of her as well. At that point, she had lived for eighty-two years and never stopped loving, caring, or giving to anyone as long as I had known her.

I knew just how proud she was of me because she knew I was shy, yet she lavished me with compliments every chance she had. She had gotten much older now and expressed even more pride in my achievements. Therefore, her praise and compliments didn't bother me anymore. I loved that she felt good about it. At this point, anything that gave her comfort put me over the moon.

Spending so much time with her allowed me time to reflect on our time together. And with plenty of practice, I had done something that I could never manage over the years:

I managed to say, ***"I love you, Mom."***

I walked out each day feeling proud and victorious about it—I had conquered a necessary fear: telling my mom that I loved her each time I walked out her door.

When I heard she was sick, I was in denial. I would always get mad and accuse her of being a hypochondriac. However, I think she saw right through it. She knew that my anger was a smokescreen shielding my fears of losing her.

When she turned 83 years old, I was still in denial and refused to accept that she would ever get sick and leave us. I knew she couldn't live forever, but at this point, I held out hope that she was an exception

to the rule of life. She had managed almost forty years since the loss of my dad.

Even in her older age, she loved playing poker, so often, my brother and I would go there and play poker with her. We wanted to involve her in doing what she'd always loved. We brought the entertainment to her. This was also our way of keeping her from the casino where she would be unsupervised.

It was such a pleasure to know that we brought her so much joy and laughter in her golden years.

Therefore, when the CANCER hit me, I kept it from everyone, mainly her.

CHAPTER XXXV –
THE EARLY ANXIETIES

*T*anya went with me to get a routine physical. I never thought about any lifelong illnesses and never felt sick. Although I urinated a little more than usual, this was still just a routine physical.

However, this time the doctor requested a rectal exam. I just thought he considered my age and that the time was right. Those are always uncomfortable, but it had to be done.

After he'd completed the rectal exam, the doctor requested my permission to allow another doctor and some students in. I assumed this was a learning experience for the students, and although it made me uncomfortable, I agreed to allow them in. I remember thinking to myself, "How many doctors does it take to look up my ass?"

While they studied inside me, the doctor then asked another doctor to come in. I almost screamed, "That's enough!" But now, I was curious.

There were at least four doctors in the room. When they finally left, my doctor came in alone and scheduled me for a biopsy. This could not wait, he warned.

Now, I was eerily concerned because my dad had died of cancer.

The day of the biopsy, *Tanya* and I were anxious. They called my name almost immediately. I can assure you that a single biopsy sample was worse than having a bullet hole in your leg filled with gauze and no anesthesia or numbing. I knew that feeling, and this was worse. This guy needed twelve samples. I lay there while they clipped my prostate twelve times. It was the worst pain I had ever felt in my life.

After a few days, he called us into his office to give us the results. When we arrived, the nurse ushered us into the doctor's office. He initially looked at us as if he had great news.

He smiled and said, ***"It's Cancer!"***

I stood there in disbelief. He had just delivered the most life-threatening news anyone could receive as matter-of-factly as possible? I was more flabbergasted by how he delivered the news than by the

news he actually delivered. For a moment, I forgot about the cancer and thought more about clocking this clown.

But then I thought, I've never had cancer. Maybe delivering the news like this makes us angrier than sad. Whether he purposely implemented that strategy or not, I don't know, but it worked—at least at that moment, because I don't remember being scared, only angry.

I didn't rock his clock. I simply walked out with my wife, thinking of how this was going to change my lifestyle. I knew that some things had to change. I had cancer and would have to schedule surgery soon. But later, I seriously contemplated trying to beat it without surgery.

The heart-to-heart with my wife happened when we got over the shock. We talked about what she would do, post me. To my surprise, she was handling this way better than I hoped she would. Why didn't she faint or break down?

Regardless, she showed amazing strength.

I was hurt at the thought of leaving her but felt a strange sense of relief when I thought about dying before my mother. At least I would not suffer from the loss of her.

But I never considered how devastating my loss would be to

my mother and others.

Then I thought about a conversation I had with my mom three months prior to finding out about the cancer. I admitted to her that I wanted to go before her because I could not handle it if I lost her. She looked at me with sincerity and asked me if I was crazy.

I had lost an older brother four years earlier. When he died, I was more devastated by what she was going through than by not seeing my brother again. So, I reconsidered my views.

Just then, I decided to fight with all of my might. I could not bear her going through my brother's funeral all over again—and this time, with her baby boy. So, I decided to schedule the surgery. I was going to fight to keep her from going through the loss of another son.

I scheduled the surgery as soon as possible but swore my wife to secrecy. No one was to know about this cancer or the surgery. She cried like a baby and begged me to tell my family. I didn't want anyone

(mainly my mom) going through the pain of possibly losing me, so I was adamant that she keep this a secret.

I seriously considered alternative treatments. After all, the World Health Organization linked certain processed meats and sugars to cancer. I could cut meat and sugar out of my diet. I wouldn't need treatments, let alone a dependency on long-term medications to beat this shit if it worked.

When I met with the doctors during my appointment, I had three questions for them.

Surely, one of them would tell me what I wanted to hear and put me more at ease prior to surgery. I had lost my dad to this shit and wanted to know just how far medical advancements had come since then.

As six Indian doctors sat at a table with me, I noticed two looked asleep, two were studying some trends on their computers, and the other two had their arms folded as if they were contemplating dinner and had no interest in my situation. So, as Dr. Mani Menon shared some chart trends with me about surgeries and recoveries, I asked my questions. 1. How long have I had it? 2. How fast is it spreading? And

3. If you cut me open, will it accelerate the process? As I awaited a reply, you could hear a pin drop in the room. Not one of them said shit. So, I resolved that my alternative methods had to work.

I got up and walked out of the room. As I walked down the hallway towards the exit, displeased with their reactions to my questions, one of the doctors (my primary, who was the youngest) ran after me, begging me to hear the doctor out. I listened to his reasoning. He assured me that Dr. Menon was one of the best urologists in the country and that I should please hear him out. He begged.

So, I went back.

This time, Dr. Menon was more vocal and convincing. He explained the procedure, the odds, and the trends more thoroughly this time. He concluded with an emphatic, ***"You will not beat this on your own."***

As confident as I was, he struck a nerve this time. I trusted his knowledge. Alternative treatments may have worked, but because he

delivered his last statement with such resounding conviction, I was not willing to risk it. My surgery was scheduled.

Tanya continued to cry and urged me to tell someone. Her initial reaction convinced me that she could handle me dying. She was simply

177

worried my family would blame her for not telling them if I did die.

We went through this alone for about five months. So, I advised her that on the day of the surgery we would tell my brother, *Old Man.*

During the surgery, *Tanya* cried and disappeared into the lobby when they wheeled me back. I was put in a room where they, again, explained to me where the incision would be as they shaved my private area and my lower stomach.

As a beautiful nurse started to shave my groin area, it became a little embarrassing when I began to get a hard-on. I think it had more to do with the tickling sensation than her beauty. Nevertheless, I felt uncomfortable. It was like I was cheating on my wife. I was glad she wasn't there. However, she may have found it humorous and laughed it off had she been there.

The doctor made one last visit while I was conscious. He shook my hand and said, *"You're going to be fine."* As he turned to walk away, I called him back. He put his hand on my arm, and I looked at him sincerely, with watery eyes, and asked if I could be the most important person in his life today.

He waited, as if pondering a response then said, *"You are!"*

I was ready to go under.

Suddenly, I was wheeled into an all-white room. *Dr. Menon* was nowhere in sight. I asked the anesthesiologist where the doctor was, and he pointed to a room and advised me that the doctor would perform the surgery from there. I was confused and asked how he was going to perform surgery from all the way over there. He said, *"He's going to perform the surgery operating that robot,"* then gestured to the corner where the robot looked slumped over.

I was both shocked and pleased. I thought about the third question I asked the doctor while sitting in that room weeks earlier: "If you cut me open, will the cancer accelerate?" I no longer had that

concern. There would only be a one-inch incision to bring out the cancerous organ. He had decided to do robotic surgery.

When I woke up, after nine hours of surgery, I was in a room with five family members. I was shocked and told *Tanya* she could not hold water. Nobody was supposed to know except *Old Man*.

She assured me that she phoned them after the surgery, so I forgave her.

I was happy to see them and happy I made it through. Strangely, though, I thought about my mother's fragility at that very moment. Her words stuck with me. In our deepest conversation, we spoke of how blessed she was to see all her kids reach and surpass the wonderful age of fifty years.

She assured me months earlier that she had to die before me because I had so much more to live for. She reminded me that people were relying on me. I accepted that, but I was still deeply saddened by her sudden fragility. My extremely independent mother was now struggling to get up and down the stairs.

I recovered so well that I requested to leave the hospital early. I was scheduled for two more days, but I explained that I had a great wife who would look after me at home.

They agreed and released me. I stopped over at my mom's and started throwing around a basketball with the kids on the streets.

I wanted her to see this and know that I was feeling great. She was amazed and thankful that I had made it through and was healthy again. When the pain medication wore off, I regretted playing basketball. I was aching fiercely.

My doctor followed my progress and knew I was doing well. So, when I called the hospital to renew my narcotics, *Dr. Menon* called my cell phone directly and told me that I was in no pain and didn't need the meds. I confirmed his suspicions and canceled the order. He was amazing.

A year after the surgery, I received an invitation from *Dr. Menon* and the Henry Ford team to attend a Top Golf Luncheon at the casino to speak to some of the Detroit Lions players about my cancer journey.

I thought about it for a while but refused. I was going through enough and didn't want to answer questions from a bunch of healthy rich kids feeling sorry for me.

Six months later, I got the invitation again through an email. The doctor's secretary implored me to attend. So, this time, I did.

There were a couple of kids there to meet the players when I showed up. One kid followed me around the entire time I was there. We talked about dating and played golf together for about an hour. He expressed to me that he'd only dated one girl his entire life. I thought it was wonderful.

As we sat and ate, I expressed my concern about the players not arriving on time. He laughed and looked at me. I didn't get the joke.

Then he said, *"We've been here."* I looked at him and asked his name again. He said, *"Andrew ... Andrew Jones."* Then he pointed out some other players. They looked no older than seventeen. We had a great laugh about that.

As we sat at the table, the players asked a few questions, and I answered. As a few girls circled the table, I asked the players how they resisted all the temptations and pitfalls of being pro athletes? A few of them laughed and said, *"Unlike other athletes, we wear helmets,"* then continued, *"No one knows who we are if we don't tell them."*

I thought that player was naïve. I expressed that women are clever. They do reconnaissance on you when you pull up in a one-hundred-thousand-dollar car. I warned them that some women would probably know who they were even before the second date.

After they shared the positions they played on the team, they laughed and shared their humor about *Andrew's* love life situation as if he wasn't sitting at the table right next to me.

They teased him about the fact that he hadn't been able to enjoy the celebrity side of life and date other women. This was because he'd been with his girlfriend since elementary school. They teased him because he had never been with another woman. They continued, ***"We told him to enjoy himself first, then get married."***

I was embarrassed for him and chimed in, ***"Well, I think Andy's pretty smart. He knows who he is with,"*** I continued. ***"He won't***

end up with someone he thought loved him, only to find out ... after two or three kids, that she never really loved him," I concluded. ***"I personally think he's the luckiest guy at the table."***

Needless to say, they weren't fans of mine after that. And I probably couldn't convince them that robotic surgery is the way to go, but I didn't care. I had made a true friend. *Andy* walked me to the valet afterward and waited until my car arrived, then waved and watched me drive off.

He had just been traded from the Jacksonville Jaguars and was coming off the injured reserve list at that time. He was working his way back into the starting lineup. I wished him well and advised him that, no matter what, wonderful things seemed destined for him. He was a good kid.

CHAPTER XXXVI – MY TREATMENTS

Four years later, COVID-19 ran rampant through the world, and its detailed effects were rarely known. Also, my cancer came back in March of 2020. Talk about bad timing.

Hospitals were accepting emergency patients and appointments only. Makeshift mobile units were serving as small medical centers outside hospital facilities. Nurses and doctors alike expressed heroism and fear. I was so proud of them during this chaos.

My doctor scheduled radiation treatment for me. However, with all the chaos at the hospitals, it would be almost impossible for me to get in and out of the hospital daily for two months of treatments.

So, due to the COVID-19 craze, my treatments were scheduled for later that year.

Rather than have me coming back and forth to the hospital during this chaotic time, my doctor and I rolled the dice.

He suggested I get a hormone shot that would slow the cancer for the following six months. This would prevent me from being at the hospital during these crazy times. I would have to come back after the summer on a date yet to be determined for these treatments.

The doctor warned me that one of the side effects of the hormone treatment was hot flashes. But he assured me that I wouldn't grow breasts, so I was satisfied and got the shot. I thought to myself, women have hot flashes all the time. I could deal with it for five or six months—no big deal—or so I thought!

Other than the biopsy, the hot flashes were the worst things I'd ever experienced. Once the biopsy was completed within an hour or so, it was over. The hot flashes went on continuously for six or seven months.

I've always had respect for women. And basically, all of them experience hot flashes in their lives at one time or another. I say this with all sincerity: After experiencing them firsthand, I now have a new level of respect for women that I thought was not possible.

These feelings were devastating. I was literally putting my head in the freezer and breathing in ten-minute intervals. I hate summers because of the 90-degree-plus days.

And now, I had a horrible hot summer day trapped inside me, randomly using me to exude heat rays.

The perfect comparison to hot flashes is when they inject you with iodine, then insert you in that X-ray machine to scan your bones. You feel nauseated. It feels like your body is heating faster than a microwave. I felt like the Agent from The Matrix must have felt when *Keanu Reeves* jumped into his body, realizing he was **The One** ... It felt like I was going to explode.

When I complained about the hot flashes to *Tanya*, she grinned and said, ***"You'll be alright."*** It gave me strength knowing she was experiencing them as well. I may have made it through the cancer without her, but I don't think I could have made it through the hot flashes without her.

Women, I tip my hat to you every day.

The radiation treatments were scheduled every weekday for eight weeks. They were from late July through August of 2020.

I had to enter Henry Ford's Radiation Oncology Department in West

183

Bloomfield through the back door of the hospital. There was rarely any waiting time, and the treatments lasted about five minutes apiece.

The staff was one of a kind. They were always so nice and courteous to all of us going through that back door and fighting for our lives.

I had seen some doctors and nurses in hospitals during this COVID outbreak who expressed a lot of fear and concern. They appeared overly cautious coming near patients. When you consider how scared the patients must have been, it had to make the doctor-patient relationship a bit uncomfortable and a little strained.

This group showed no fear and made us feel like COVID did not exist. This team seemed to love every patient who entered their doors and they expressed it. If I had to die from cancer, that would have been

where I wanted to expire. They expressed no fear and only love and concern. Their actions and skills provided true comfort.

After the ringing of the bell signaling my completion, I brought them bags of Lindt chocolates as a small token of my appreciation. I also wrote them a touching tribute following my last radiation treatment to express my feelings about my time spent with them:

8/21/2020

HENRY FORD RADIATION & ONCOLOGY STAFF

My True Heroes,

Words cannot express the appreciation I have for each and every one of you. Your gallant efforts put forth over the past eight weeks in prolonging my existence and providing comfort to all of us who face cancer, COVID-19, and other debilitating illnesses do not go unnoticed.

I truly understand that your efforts are no small feat and that you may think you are often taken for granted, but you're not. Most of us come to understand that you zip, button, and lace up to report for duty on a daily basis, regardless of what awaits you ... sort of like those represented in the Justice League.

Most of us recognize the profile of true heroes: they sacrifice themselves; they are unselfish with their time and actions; they share their knowledge regardless of race, age, and other differences; they comfort the less fortunate while continuously serving them; they stay focused on their positive contributions to the world, even during trying times and in challenging environments; they display inclusion and bipartisanship to those in their care (a blueprint for world leaders). You fit the profile!

In my book, there are truly eight wonders of this world, the latter being not only modern medicine but also those who research, practice, implement, and follow up on its shared effects with the world. I am fortunate to be one of the many recipients of these discoveries.

Not only am I thrilled to be a beneficiary of these findings and practices, but I am overwhelmed at the possibility that my

treatments are part of the study that links today's science with tomorrow's discoveries and treatments—continuously strengthening and lengthening the lives of others.

If your recent efforts have pushed my existence just one day past my original expiration date, you have performed yet another miracle, and I am truly grateful knowing that it will benefit the next patient and those thereafter.

In parting, I leave you with words of wisdom and encouragement, in hopes of keeping your hearts beating strong and your minds racing toward your daily endeavors:

"The finest qualities of our characters do not come from trying but from that mysterious and yet most effective capacity to be inspired."

—Harry Emerson Fosdick

Thank you, Larry D. Snell

CANCER SURVIVOR

I asked them to wait until I left before they read it. I was too touched at the thought of their commitment to helping others and the thought of me leaving my friends.

CHAPTER XXXVII –
MY LOSSES

A s far as I was concerned, my team and I beat cancer. My mom was so happy. I thought about our conversations months ago, and it hit me that she would probably be leaving before me.

Therefore, I visited her as much as I could. My dog and I sat with her in her room on Saturday mornings. She would reminisce about her grandfather and others she loved, as if they were there with us. She laughed and shared some of their fun stories. It worried me that she began reminiscing so far in the past, but she was comfortable, and I listened.

When my brother called me at 12 p.m. and told me she was in the hospital, I panicked.

He said she was feeling fine but needed surgery. I felt numb. The doctor said the surgery could extend her life for a week or for a year—it was hard to tell.

I got out of bed and told *Tanya* that I was on my way to the hospital. *Old Man* advised me that she was going to be airlifted to the University of Michigan Medical Center for the surgery.

I cried and said I would meet them in Ann Arbor. I knew my mom was always afraid of flying and rarely accepted vacation gifts that involved flying.

Turns out, she refused the helicopter and was rushed by ambulance to U of M Medical Center.

She died en route.

My mom died a few months following my radiation treatments and one month after her 84th birthday. A month later, I lost my oldest nephew, Justin, in a rollover accident on I-696. I was devastated. I once asked him why he tattooed my names on his arm and he said, **"Because I love you,"** then looked at me with the shyness of a school kid and said, **"I want to be married like my Uncle Larry, too."**

I couldn't cry in front of him, so I went home and wept at the thought of his admiration for me.

Within a span of five months, I battled cancer for the second time ..I suddenly lost my mother to heart failure ... and my nephew's brakes went out on his minivan, killing him on the I-696 freeway.

And, as if I hadn't gone through enough, two months later, *Tanya* advised me that she wanted a divorce. I thought this was a distasteful joke. But it wasn't. I had hit rock bottom.

After fifteen years of marriage, she said she wanted to live again. I didn't know how to feel. I had physically died after my surgery.

I struggled with intimacy and barely managed at all, so I understood life was suddenly different for her, but I was still alive and optimistic.

I held off the divorce for two months, begging and pleading, but I was going through way too much to grovel anymore. And besides, I always wanted to see her happy, so if it took a divorce to make her genuinely happy again, I couldn't hold her back.

I filed for divorce to give her what she wanted. I wasn't going to keep her in a marriage she didn't want anymore. Nothing was contested, and the divorce was final. Oddly enough, I understood her struggles, but mine were just beginning.

My attorney was so pissed that I didn't go after her assets and alimony that he came after mine. In the end, I negotiated his payoff and finalized our deal. I had nothing.

My ex-wife and I had to live together until the house was sold. We got a lot of views at our open house events, but no takers. Living together was getting testy. I was still concerned about her well-being, yet she began coming home much later than she ever had. And I thought she was afraid of the dark all these years.

I grew impatient and had enough. THIS HOUSE WAS GOING TO SELL! I woke up one day like a man possessed. I painted the entire interior of the house. I replaced the broken marble in the foyer. I even replaced the baseboards around the basement.

I called the realtor when I was done and scheduled another open house. This time we got five offers within the week. We didn't take the highest offer but the median one—I wanted this deal done without a hitch!'

Our signing was on Thursday. I hoped to see my ex-wife one last time before we parted ways for good and finalized our official business. Sure, there were testy moments, but we were cordial, nonetheless. So, I wanted to see her before everything was concluded.

After work, I called her to time our arrival at the realtor's office and got no answer. Turns out she had other plans.

To my surprise, she had gone into the realtor's office and signed her portion of the paperwork on Wednesday (one day prior) and had relocated to Florida by Thursday (signing day). My marriage was over, and an enormous feeling of sadness began to settle in.

To make matters worse, the realtor contacted me prior to signing the sales document to tell me that 80% of the one-hundred-twenty-thousand dollars profit awarded to me from the sale of the house went to Fannie Mae. I had no idea about the subordinate mortgage taken out on the property six years prior.

I didn't bother to call my attorney about this matter. I settled for what was left.

Now, I was basically broke, divorced, and recovering from so much heartache that I didn't have the strength to battle anymore.

CHAPTER XXXVIII – THE AFTERMATH

After everything I had gone through, my optimism and faith had never wavered. I tried to find hobbies to keep me occupied.

My neighbor was in the music promotion business and had a few artists in Africa that he represented. I don't know how he managed that long-distance business thing, but it worked for him.

So, when he asked me to co-host a morning radio talk show with him, I was ecstatic. I was doing modest home improvement projects with a management company and had plenty of time to co-host the show, so I agreed.

On the show, we conversed daily events, and I even hosted a current events news segment. I brought in some local talent for interviews and to get their perspectives on social issues. My partner was impressed with the guests I brought in.

After about three months on air, *Bill Bonds* and *Rich Fisher* wanted our 10 a.m. time slot on the station and got it. These were two over-the-hill titans of the local television news industry where I once worked.

Both had worked as anchors where I started my news career. Just like that, my broadcasting career was over. But it kept me busy and masked some of the sadness I was feeling. It bought me some time and it was fun while it lasted.

I kept as busy as I could. Buddy, my dog, became my best friend. He had gone through all the heartache I had recently experienced. My trusted companion was right there and seemed to mimic my sadness during the loss of my mom, my nephew, the cancer, and the divorce.

He loved my mother as much as I did. I had taken him everywhere, and he never left my side. I guess he was worried I would leave him wherever we went. However, while visiting Mom, he would run upstairs to her bedroom and wake her up if she appeared to be asleep.

She often toyed with him, hiding under her blanket and pretending she wasn't there. He would then place his front paws on

the bed and try to sniff her out. She laughed and gave herself away every time. When I went upstairs, he would always sit on the floor next to her house shoes. He was never concerned about me leaving him there.

My brother still lived in my mom's old house. Buddy and I would occasionally visit him. And for the longest time, Buddy would go upstairs and sit by her bed where her house shoes once were. But lately, he looks around, sniffs, then comes back downstairs and sits next to me. He knows that the game between them has ended.

After my cancer surgery, he never plays rough with me anymore but always lays his head on my lap and stares at me. It's amazing to see this shift in his personality. It honestly feels as if he knows what I've gone through.

With so much free time, I began taking him to Belle Isle, where I would watch him chase ducks and geese along the river's edge. He once jumped into the river while following a flock of geese. I nearly jumped in after him. But he found the shallow spot on the shore and came back. I honestly think I would have jumped in and swam after him had the current taken him under. He was my best and only faithful companion.

I never wanted to be pitied by anyone and accepted my fate— whatever it was. But Buddy pities me, and I can't make him stop ...

lol.

I have done everything within my power to stay alive and have no further control over what happens to me. So now, I'm doing a lot of reflection and writing. I love fantasy and write quite a bit of it. Then I read it to awaken a magical feeling within me. It gives me joy. Then I toss it aside and rarely view it again. I repeat the process to feel alive again.

I began to write poetry and short stories again. I am always pleased with the results. I think to myself, "You still got it!" I am still able to express and record my feelings through my material, and it is very necessary at this stage.

CHAPTER XXXIX – PASSING ALONG ONE FINAL REFLECTION

There are few regrets that I have in my life. One, in particular, stands out: my decision not to attend Middlebury College. My narrow-mindedness kept me from attending a college that *Robert Frost, Toni Morrison, James Cromwell, Jake Weber, Emily McLaughlin*, and a few other renowned authors had attended.

However, although I have this regret, and a few others, I do not think I would change a thing in my life if given the chance. Even cancer is a lesson learned and contributes to the pillars of strength I rely on while I live.

The lesson in life that I would give to anyone is to know that life is like a hobbit's tale:

You are there and back again. It is to be reflected upon.

Write down your journeys, your emotions, and your passions to draw upon later in life. I promise you that if you do, you will be pleased with the sound, solid decisions you make in your life. Do it so that you do not forget who you were at those moments. You will have a clearer vision of who you are in the present.

To tell it all, my epithet need only read: "He lived through it all and loved anyway."

I leave you my truth to be inspired:

I have never been, so I'll go.

I have not heard, so I'll listen.

I have never shed a tear, so I'll cry.

I have not had the chance, and do not know why.

I am where, stiff as a painting ... judge of color and beauty,
With no true admirers.

The sun's heat,

Melting my elements, causing landslides,

Till all of me pours into already polluted lakes, flowing to no
destination of even time.

I am creating massive damage, widespread ... And can only
hear as I am being collected;

Panic settling ashore ... fearing the fish are in danger, Yet
knowing ... that the only endangered species is I.

As hope fades ...

I see the shore. I gather every ounce of strength within me

... and reach out with what is left of me –

To go ... where I have not gone. To hear ... what I have not
heard.

And to shed a tear ... for even asking why!

— Larry D. Snell

Just go for it! Do what you are passionate about and don't be deterred. Others aren't meant to live your life for you. But you owe it to yourself to be true to yourself and live the life meant for you.